In Reasonable Hope

IN REASONABLE HOPE

Philosophical Reflections on
Ultimate Meaning

Patrick Masterson

The Catholic University of America Press
Washington, D.C.

Library of Congress Cataloging-in-Publication Data
Names: Masterson, Patrick, author.
Title: In reasonable hope : philosophical reflections on ultimate meaning /
Patrick Masterson.
Description: Washington, D.C. : The Catholic University of America Press, [2021] |
Includes bibliographical references and index.
Identifiers: LCCN 2020057635 | ISBN 9780813233864 (paperback)
Subjects: LCSH: Meaning (Philosophy) | Humanism. | Scientism. | Theism.
Classification: LCC B105.M4 M383 2021 | DDC 121/.68—dc23
LC record available at https://lccn.loc.gov/2020057635

*For my beloved Frankie
and my former students*

Contents

CONTENTS

INTRODUCTION

We live in the most developed society in the history of the world, technologically and even culturally, but this very development allows us to ignore a curious question: "What does it all ultimately mean?" We live out our lives, in all their monochrome and colorful moments, not always as well as we might but at least in an engaging and often very agreeable manner. However, we do so against an unattended but not entirely unexperienced backdrop of ultimate meaning. Occasionally, by reflecting or maybe only accidentally noticing, we catch a glimpse of this background and are brought to a momentary disconcerting interruption of our complacent "everydayness," an interruption from which we usually quickly and adeptly disengage ourselves. Because on that backdrop is inscribed unavoidably in bold letters that question: "WHAT DOES IT ALL ULTIMATELY MEAN?" Is reality ultimately contingent, meaningless, chaotic, and repellent? Or is it intrinsically dependable, truthful, good, and beautiful? If it is meaningful, why? How so?

When we take a moment to disengage from our screens and our constant list of daily tasks, we find ourselves existing as incarnate subjects in a physical world with other people. We claim some comprehension of the law-like operation of the fundamental particles of which this world is composed and of its historical development and evolution. We seek to arrange our practical communication and commerce with other people in what we believe to be a rational, humane, and equitable manner. We marvel at the remarkable, and occasionally infamous, development of human civilization since its earliest origin to our own enlightened age. We reflect upon its historically developed institutions—economic, scientific, moral, political, cultural, and religious. We wonder what all of this means, asking how and even why it has come to pass. Is human existence itself the fundamental phenomenon in terms of which all reality, all meaning, all value, must be ultimately understood and explained? Or is the universe, including human existence, to be ultimately understood less anthropocentrically, in exclusively impersonal scientific terms? Is it at bottom an amazing natural, inexorable, or highly probable and scientifically comprehensible development from an initial inexplicable explosion into existence of a conglomeration of law-like orderly activities and operations of basic physical particles? Or is there perhaps some even more fundamental explanation of the existence, meaning, and value of everything?

Instead of discreetly, or perhaps even perplexedly, turning away from this basic backdrop question, I want to dwell upon it—notwithstanding a dismissive remark typical of contemporary philosophers that today "no one of any discretion writes about the Universe, Man, and God."[1] It is at least worth considering why this dismissal might seem "obvious" to us now, and whether it is a well-founded conviction or just a widespread assumption.

In this book, I will first consider various foundational responses that the question has provoked. This will involve examining three main approaches to the question. Other approaches, I believe, can be viewed as variations or combinations of one or more of these three approaches. Here I want to concentrate upon the three distinct approaches to the puzzling issue of "what, in the final anal-

1. Rom Harre, *Philosophies of Science* (Oxford: Oxford University Press, 1970), 8.

ysis, is the ultimate meaning and value of being in general and of human existence in particular?"

First, there is the approach that maintains that our human reality, in the exercise of its unique and remarkable conscious subjectivity, is the ultimate source and measure of what can be affirmed about the meaning and value of everything, including ourselves. Our unique human condition is taken to be the focal source and unsurpassable cradle of all possible meaning and value. Our intentional relationship to the world and to other people, and their correlative presence to our consciousness, enables and constitutes the defining and exclusive context in which the quest for ultimate meaning and value must be pursued. In support of this claim, one can indicate the evident truth that, for us humans, nothing can be thought of as existing, meaningful, or of value apart from a thinking human subject. Even the affirmations of physical science or the expressions of religious belief are ultimately rooted in the astonishing cognitive resource of our human subjectivity. All our affirmations of meaning and value are intrinsically correlative to this human conscious subjectivity. This approach, which represents a specific and influential form of the wider notion of humanism, I call correlationist humanism.

Second, there is the approach that claims that the ultimate meaning and value of everything, insofar as this can be known, is to be sought not in terms of some all-embracing humanist vision but scientifically in terms of the objective findings of basic empirical sciences such as physics, chemistry, and biology. It is in terms of these findings that the evolution and existence of human subjectivity itself must, insofar as it is possible, be ultimately understood and explained. This approach can take two distinctive forms, which I call scientism and scientific naturalism. Scientism is an explicitly reductionist and materialist conception of the meaning and value of everything. Scientific naturalism involves recognition of the irreducible significance of the mind but only as a feature of the material universe amenable to empirical scientific comprehension.

Third, there is the approach that holds that, in the final analysis, the meaning and value of everything, insofar as this can be known, is to be elucidated in terms of a profoundly mysterious transcendent reality "to which everyone gives the name of God."[2] The experienced universe and all that it encompasses by way of intelligibility and value, including our human existence, are ultimately to be understood as the benevolent creation of a deeper or higher reality, a God of infinite perfection and goodness. This approach is described as theism. It finds expression, as we shall see, in two main forms. It can be formulated as a philosophical viewpoint that developed at least somewhat independent of any particular religious tradition (in the Greeks Plato and Aristotle) and has been held ever since as a tenet of natural reason alone by at least some thinkers who did not adhere to any particular faith.[3] Or it can find expression in various forms of religious belief as revealed truth, accessible in virtue of a divine gift of faith that greatly exceeds what may be known about God by natural reason alone.

Although these three approaches are very different in their fundamental perspectives, they can impinge upon one another to some extent. However interesting such interrelationships may be, I propose to consider them only briefly and incidentally—for example, in my discussion of the relationship between scientific naturalism and humanism. I concentrate centrally on the three clearly distinct

2. Thomas Aquinas, *Summa theologiae*, trans. English Dominicans (London: Eyre and Spottiswoode, 1964–74) I, q. 2, a. 3.

3. The existence of God as a part of natural reason has also been debated among religious thinkers: that is to say, "what ought those with no religious revelation know about God?"

approaches to the great question of the ultimate meaning and value of being in general and of human existence in particular. In other words I will take humanism, scientism and scientific naturalism, and theism as signifying very different approaches to ultimate meaning and value, as indeed they do: three basic responses to the question "What does it all ultimately mean?"

As may be surmised from my disproportionate attention to the theistic viewpoint, I must declare at the outset that theism is the view that, on reflection and careful consideration, I personally accept as most convincing. However, it is important to emphasize that the other viewpoints are very widely held with equal sincerity and genuine intellectual conviction. That this is so is perhaps paradoxical. However, it needs to be borne in mind by all engaged in the discussion. For it has social and personal consequences concerning how we should value and respect one another. It also encourages us to review attentively the considerations that support approaches other than the one that we personally accept and to reflect on what bearing these considerations may have upon our own conclusions.

Although this reflection is intended for the educated nonspecialist reader, some of the early part (chapters 1 to 6) inevitably involves some rather abstract philosophical ideas, which I try to elucidate in more readily comprehensible terms. The second part (chapters 7 to 18) is expressed in more commonplace personal idiom and introduces some familiar theological considerations, but still in a philosophical mode (there will be no proof-texting here). It enjoys a measure of autonomy vis-à-vis the earlier philosophical ruminations; it is more personally focused and represents a shift in orientation from impersonal theoretical argument to self-involving rational hope. While, as I have already noted, there have been thinkers from the dawn of Western philosophy who have found compelling the impersonal theoretical arguments for theism, I would suggest that most people in general, and especially most people today, are better served to also consider the full gamut of theistic intellectual reflections, which involve not only a God who reveals himself as love but also one's own self that reveals itself as made for such love—certainly this would be the path that some humanists have taken to reach theism.

Indeed, the second half of the book could be considered separately, and perhaps some readers would rather not have to work through the "abstract" ideas of the first half. However, the work is conceived as a unified reflection, and I think the earlier deliberations provide a relevant and valuable theoretical context or complement for the subsequent more personal deliberations. In addition to the general casting aside of questions of meaning, to which I referred at the outset of this introduction, too many people in contemporary culture still gesture towards "spiritual" meaning in a vague way that cannot bear rational scrutiny. As any professor who has taught contemporary Western undergraduates religion or philosophy could tell you, the tendency to ignore rational considerations in this realm produces a degree of muddle-headed thinking that would be embarrassing and unacceptable if applied to any other discipline. This is not to try, as some authors do, to fit the round peg of ultimate meaning into the square hole of precise definitions and methodological limitations best suited to the physical sciences. Rather, I simply encourage any reader who encounters this book to embrace willingly both the abstract and the concrete, the theoretical and the personal, as two complementary approaches to the same reality. I hope that everyone who reads this book—especially theists who may find their reasons for hope expanded and confirmed—will grow in their capacity to think more clearly about "What does it all ultimately mean?," and will look more sympathetically towards those who answer this question differently from themselves.

One

CORRELATIONIST HUMANISM

In this chapter I want to outline the view that human life, such as each of us individually enjoys as an incarnate subject in a world with other people, provides the englobing and fundamental context for a discussion of the ultimate meaning and value of being in general and of human existence in particular. Its animating principle is the claim originally attributed to Protagoras in the fifth century BC that "man is the measure of all things." This is not my own view, but it is an important one.

Humanism is the term widely adopted to describe this viewpoint, and it is understood as focusing attention centrally, exclusively, and irreducibly upon human beings and their conscious abilities, significations, objectives, and values. Originally, in Classical Greek and later in Renaissance thought, the notion of "humanism" had other and looser connotations. It could, for example, signify practical philanthropic concern for one's fellow humans or reflective dedication to the study and pursuit of classical literature or the liberal arts (much as we still refer to the "humanities"). As such, it was usually perceived as quite compatible with religious faith—thus the "humanist" scholar Erasmus was a committed Christian. It could also signify a measure of self-assertion and rebellion vis-à-vis the control of human destiny by the whims of the gods, as demonstrated in the myth of Prometheus's punishment for the theft of the divine resource of fire from the gods.

Although these traditional understandings still have some resonance, in more modern and contemporary usage "humanism" is usually understood as expressing an uncompromisingly anthropocentric and secular view on life. Although it values human scientific achievement, this humanism claims to avoid, on the one hand, the pitfalls of "scientific" reductive depersonalization and, on the other, any extraneous theistic interpretation of the human condition. The American Humanist Association, whose slogan is "Good Without God," defines humanism in the following terms: "Humanism is a progressive philosophy of life that, without theism or other supernatural beliefs, affirms our ability and responsibility to lead ethical lives of personal fulfillment that aspire to the greater good of humanity."[1] According to Bette Chambers, former president of the association, "All human life must seek a reason for existence within the bounds of an uncaring physical world, and it is love coupled with empathy, democracy, and commitment to selfless service which undergirds the faith of a humanist."[2]

According to humanism, humanity is to be understood rigorously, comprehensively, and exclusively in terms proper to itself. This involves affirming that it is characterized by a form of personal autonomy and distinctively first-person qualities of subjectivity and intersubjectivity whereby everything that might be known, affirmed, or valued is uniquely and inescapably correlated with human consciousness. Humankind, thus understood, cannot be adequately considered or described in impersonal objective terms

---

1. "Definition of Humanism," American Humanist Association, accessed February 26, 2020, https://americanhumanist.org/what-is-humanism/definition-of-humanism/.
    2. Ibid.

in the way in which, for example, the movement of the planets might be.

The humanism in which this conception of humanity finds expression has been associated with various cultural movements which view the human condition as the ultimate value and the central and basic object of philosophical attention. It is characteristic not just of classical Greek and Renaissance thought but also, more recently, of movements such as the nineteenth-century optimistic rationalism of Feuerbach ("the *absolute* to man is his own nature") and the more pessimistic twentieth-century existentialism of Jean-Paul Sartre ("existentialism is humanism"). Indeed, it can also be seen as the animating principle, the *point de repère*, of much of contemporary continental European phenomenology and Anglo-American linguistic philosophy (as different as those two strands of philosophy can be). It is with a consideration of this more recent philosophical conception of humanism, which I call correlationist humanism, that I will be principally concerned.

Since modern times the animating philosophical principle of this humanism has been the persistent effort to draw out in a consistent way the implications of Rene Descartes's "Cogito ergo sum" ("I think therefore I am"), which is generally viewed as the foundation stone of modern and contemporary philosophy. This effort involves a principle that seeks to ground all meaning and value in the conscious presence of the thinking subject to herself. Descartes himself, it should be said, envisioned this revolutionary initiative not as a replacement for God but as a novel method to move from the human subject to find the ground of all meaning and value in the existence of God, which he established through recourse to his own clear and distinct idea of God as infinite being. Nevertheless, perhaps despite Descartes's wishes, this relocation of the ground of all meaning and value gave impetus to the subsequent course of European philosophy as a debate about the coexistence of God and man and about to which of these alternatives ultimate significance should be attributed. As Sartre expressed the unfolding drama: "It took two centuries of crisis—a crisis of Faith and a crisis of Science—for man to regain the creative freedom that Descartes placed in God, and for anyone to finally suspect the following truth, which is an essential basis of humanism: man is the being as a result of whose appearance a world exists."[3]

This sentiment was also emphatically expressed by Karl Marx, whose philosophy is an explicit affirmation of humanism. Thus, he claims that "religion is only the illusory sun about which man revolves so long as he does not revolve about himself." He insists that effective human emancipation is possible only "if one adopts the point of view of that theory according to which man is the highest being for man."[4]

However, the key figure in the transition preceded both Sartre and Marx. It was Immanuel Kant in the eighteenth century who removed the ambiguity in Descartes's philosophy by reaffirming more radically that all meaning and value derive from our theoretical and practical human cognitive activity. This obtains, on the one hand, in virtue of our imposition of sensory forms of space and time and categories of our understanding (such as "unity," "necessity," and "causality") on the raw unintelligible data of our experience and, on the other hand, from our own human promulgation of autonomous moral imperatives to ourselves.

3. Jean-Paul Sartre, "Cartesian Freedom," in *Literary and Philosophical Essays*, trans. Annette Michelson (London: Hutchinson, 1969), 184.

4. Karl Marx, *Contribution to the Critique of Hegel's Philosophy of Right: Early Writings*, trans T. B. Bottomore (London: C.A. Watts, 1963), 44, 59.

It is widely maintained that, since Kant's radical modification of Descartes's initiative, philosophy has characteristically refused to entertain any claim to know anything about how things are in themselves independent of our awareness of them. The strict correlation between being and human thought is affirmed as an absolute first principle (even though, as we shall see later in this study, Kant himself conceded that although God's independent existence could not be affirmed as an object of knowledge, God could be validly affirmed as an object of belief or rational hope).

An elegant and critical exposition of this conviction about the strict correlation between being and human thought is provided by Quentin Meillassoux in his interesting book *After Finitude*. He argues effectively that "the central notion of modern philosophy since Kant seems to be that of *correlation*. By 'correlation' we mean the idea according to which we only ever have access to the correlation between thinking and being, and never to either term considered apart from the other."[5] Intrinsic to this contention is the claim that we never know anything about the world as it exists independently in itself but always and only as it appears to us as a conscious subject.

This primacy of the idea of correlation is not equivalent to a claim that we are only aware of our various images or "representations" of real being. It is to claim a certain "copropriation" of thought and being, which Heidegger refers to as *Ereignis*—a correlative appearing together of being and consciousness as that which they are. It signifies that human thought and extra-mental being, although distinct, may never be affirmed as subsisting independently in themselves. They each obtain, or are constituted, only through their reciprocal relation.[6] Relationship, not self-existing "individual substance," is affirmed as the fundamental category of all reality. Being and thought do not subsist independently prior to entry into their mutual relationship. Both occur and are constituted through their reciprocal relation.

In a realist philosophy, our primary affirmation of anything as a being or as an existing reality is to affirm it as that which exists in itself, independently of our awareness and affirmation of it. This denial of a realist philosophy identifies being as essentially and only a correlate of human thought. It is this correlation that constitutes the epistemological foundation of a strict philosophical conception of humanism, a foundation quite different to that which characterizes the viewpoint of empirical science, as we shall see. It is also, I will argue, incompatible with an adequately developed theism, although in recent times this incompatibility is widely contested.

For correlationism, whatever reality, meaning, and value that being may be said to comprise is always and only a reality, meaning, and value for human consciousness. To be is to be a correlate of human thought. Being is always and only that which is given to human consciousness, and this consciousness obtains only as consciousness of being. Neither can obtain or have any meaning or value independently of their mutual relationship. Human consciousness is always openness to being—but to being that is always and only relative to human consciousness.

Everything is given to consciousness as "other" or "outside"—but an outside to which we cannot get out. As Meillassoux remarks:

It could be that contemporary philosophers have lost the *great* outdoors, the absolute outside of pre-critical thinkers: that outside which is not

6. Ibid., 8.

relative to us, and which was given as indifferent to its own givenness to be what it is, existing in itself regardless of whether we are thinking of it or not; that outside which thought could explore with the legitimate feeling of being on foreign territory—of being entirely elsewhere.[7]

The theistic attempt to affirm the independent existence of God becomes merely a particular casualty of this insistence that we are enclosed within the correlational hermeneutical circle. This affirmation of the radical correlation of being and human consciousness provides the charter and justification for a phenomenologically based humanism according to which all meaning and value, including any affirmation of God, must be seen as essentially relative to or correlative with humankind. It provides the justification and context for the most unequivocal and uncompromising form of humanism. Hegel's claim that "without the world [i.e., human consciousness] God is not God" would seem to anticipate where phenomenology's exclusive commitment to correlationism leads.[8] As I will argue in a later chapter, Hegel's claim is precisely what Christian doctrine and a metaphysical account of creation deny. The exclusive claims of phenomenology must be tempered by the complementary perspective of realist metaphysics.

For a strict correlationalist, an affirmation of the independent existence of the world or of God may be claimed to be objectively true only in the sense of being somehow intersubjectively experientially verifiable. However, it is an affirmation whose reference cannot possibly exist in the independent manner in which it is intuitively affirmed.[9] To maintain the primacy of this humanist

7. Ibid., 7.

8. G. F. Hegel, *Lectures on the Philosophy of Religion*, vol. 1, trans. Peter C. Hodgson (Berkeley: University of California Press, 1984), 308n97.

9. Meillassoux, *After Finitude*, 16–17.

perspective implies a rejection of all affirmations about the existence and nature of anything as existing intelligibly independent of its correlation with our human consciousness. This clearly has consequences for the claims not only of theism but also of the other viewpoint that proposes itself as the ultimate perspective on all issues of ultimate meaning and value, namely, empirical science. Let us consider why this is so, leaving aside for the moment any consideration of more ecumenical attempts to accommodate hybrid versions of scientific humanism.

As Meillassoux argues, accepting a strict correlationist conception of the relationship between human consciousness and being implies a rather unconventional view of the nature of empirical science. It implies that the objectivity of scientific statements about any reality no longer refers to the nature of such a reality as it is in itself but rather to the universal verifiability of such statements. For the correlationist, scientific statements are said to be objective because the relevant experimental procedures upon which they are based are intersubjectively verifiable by any member of the scientific community.[10] A particular scientific claim can be said to be objectively true because, in principle, any scientist can confirm that claim by repeating the appropriate experimental procedure. Objective truth becomes an epistemological attribute of cognitive performance rather than the correspondence of a judgment to an independently real state of affairs. Objective truth becomes a matter of intersubjective accord about how things are related to us rather than an affirmation of the conformity of our judgments with how things are in themselves.

Adopting such a strictly humanist or correlationist approach poses a particular difficulty for certain kinds of scientific claims—

10. Ibid., 15.

namely, those that Meillassoux calls "ancestral statements." Ancestral statements are the sort of statements which scientists such as astrophysicists, geologists, or paleontologists use when discussing the date of the accretion of the earth or the date of the appearance of prehuman species. What meaning can such ancestral statements have within a correlationist view of scientific knowledge? For they are statements that refer to how the world was anterior to any form of human relationship, cognitive or otherwise, to the world. What can such statements mean if all meaning is a function of the strict correlation between human thought and being? How can we say anything scientifically informative about how the world was prior to the appearance of humanity? If correlationism is true, how can scientific statements about the prehuman condition of the universe be true or even meaningful?

The correlationist humanist philosopher will concede that the scientist's spontaneously realistic interpretation of his statements, an interpretation shared with fellow scientists and nonscientists, is legitimate as a provisional way of speaking. It reflects the empirical procedure characteristic of science. According to the correlationist humanist philosopher, this scientific interpretation must, however, be corrected subsequently by the deeper level of understanding that the humanist philosopher has of the correlation between human thought and reality.

The philosopher will point out that a scientist's allegedly realistic statements about the prehuman world are in fact statements about how things appear to be for the scientist and the scientific community generally. She will insist that the scientist's statements about how the prehuman world was are relative to how such statements appear to the scientist who formulates them. What he thinks to be realistically the case is relative to his thinking it to be so. Being is *not* anterior to consciousness. It obtains only and always as *given* or *manifested* to human consciousness. As Meillassoux remarks:

> When confronted with an ancestral statement, correlationism postulates that there are at least *two levels of meaning* in such a statement: the immediate or realistic meaning, and the more originary correlationist meaning. . . . At the first, superficial level, I forget the originary nature of givenness, losing myself in the object and naturalizing givenness by turning it into a property in the physical world, one that is liable to appear and disappear in the same way as a thing (being gives itself *as anterior to givenness*). But at the deeper level (being *gives itself* as anterior to givenness) I grasp that the correlation between thought and being enjoys logical priority over every empirical statement about the world and intra-worldly entities.[11]

Thus, for example, the alleged physical prehuman ancestral existence of dinosaurs is relative to the prior and more profound correlativity of all being to human consciousness.

Various difficulties confront this strict correlationist version of humanism, which claims to disclose the ultimate meaning and value of being in general and of human existence in particular. For it commits one to various assertions that seem at least implausible. For example, an empirical scientist is unlikely to accept that his scientific claim to objective knowledge is not knowledge about real features of an independently existing world but only a claim that his experimental procedure and conclusion is intersubjectively verifiable by any member of the scientific community. He will claim that his scientifically established findings, if true, are so in virtue of how things are and not simply because the community of his fellow scientists agrees with him. He will want to maintain that his exper-

11. Ibid., 14–15.

imental procedure in addressing what is empirically given verifies a hypothesis about an aspect of how the world really is, not just of how it manifests itself to him. He will want to affirm that what he knows is how things really are in themselves, albeit not comprehensively. He will admit that our knowledge of reality is limited by the finite range of our intellectual capacity. However, he will insist that our limited knowledge, which can be progressively increased with the development of science, is knowledge of the intrinsic and independently possessed intelligibility of an extra-mental reality. As James Baggott puts it: "One of the most important features of science as a way of understanding the world is that this is inevitably an understanding *from which we are removed*.... Scientific thinking is thinking from which our own personal, subjective perspective has been eliminated."[12]

More generally, people are unlikely to accept that the intelligibility of being or reality is limited to what has been disclosed to, has been manifested to, or is strictly correlative to human consciousness. They will consider that it is more appropriate to maintain that intelligible realities obtain, and obtained in the past, and are not given or manifest to human cognition. As Shakespeare put it, "There are more things in heaven and earth, Horatio, than are dreamt of in your philosophy."[13] Most people will maintain that, while it is true to say that we know whatever we know according to our limited intellectual capacity, nevertheless this limited intellectual capacity is not the measure of the intelligibility of the reality that is known. They will maintain that while it is a simple truism that "nothing can be *thought of as existing* apart from a thinking subject," this does not mean that "nothing can be thought of *as existing*

12. Jim Baggott, *A Beginner's Guide to Reality* (London: Penguin Books, 2005), 83.
13. William Shakespeare, *Hamlet*, act 1, scene 4.

apart from a thinking subject." The latter statement is empirically false as anyone can verify for herself.

It can be argued that the relationship between being and human cognition is an asymmetrical one. In it the knower is changed and enhanced in coming to know an aspect or dimension of reality or being. The being that is known is not thereby changed or enhanced. In partially accessing its inherent intelligibility, the knowing subject is enriched, but not so the known reality. The asymmetry rather than the correlation of known and knower is the distinctive characteristic of our human knowledge of being.

Comparable considerations confront a strict correlationist humanist in addressing issues concerning ethical or moral requirements. If one accepts that human subjectivity is the root source of all meaning and value, one will seek to ground ethical or moral requirements in terms of human motivation. It will be on the basis of what motivates us that we will formulate what sort of behavior is required of us. Morality will be constituted as the behavior appropriate to satisfy what we perceive to be our human wants, desires, or motivations. People want food, so it is good both to eat and to assure that others not starve. Many thinkers in this tradition have sought to undergird traditional moral rules using the new anthropocentric worldview, much as Descartes sought to find a new proof of God beginning with his "Cogito ergo sum." But there have also been philosophers, of whom Nietzsche is a foremost exemplar, who have claimed that a thoroughgoing revision of morality "beyond good and evil" is the natural outcome of correlationism. If wealth or sexual gratification is what motivates us, why does morality not consist in adopting an uncompromising capitalism or an exploitative philandering in our dealings with others?

Such an approach ignores the consideration that there are reasons for action that are specifically and objectively moral and that really obtain irrespective of our felt needs, desires, or motivations. Ethical requirements vis-à-vis other people need not stem from a prior perceived psychological motivation, however altruistic. Rather they reveal or attain a specifically ethical motivational structure that is discerned by consideration of what a particular person or circumstance may require of us. As Thomas Nagel remarks: "There are reasons for actions which are specifically moral; it is because they represent moral requirements that they can motivate, not vice versa. If this is correct, ethics must yield discoveries about human motivation. But of what kind? Not just information about what people want. If ethics is not to presuppose any motivations, but must instead reveal their possibility, the discoveries must be at a more fundamental level than that."[14] Such considerations suggest that a viable humanism, while insisting upon the importance (and indeed irreducible significance) of human subjectivity, will have a less restrictive view of the sources of intelligibility, meaning, and value than that required by strict correlationist humanism. In particular, this more viable humanism will be disposed to accept the undeniable importance and achievement of modern science. However, while accepting the objective claims of the various sciences, it will try to integrate them into a broader humanistic perspective that promotes an understanding of objective scientific discoveries as distinctive human achievements, enabling an ever-greater realization and flourishing of human subjectivity. Indeed, it will maintain that the creation and elaboration of modern science is one of the great humanist achievements, liberating us from religious superstition and the distractions of theism and enabling us

14. Thomas Nagel, *The Possibility of Altruism* (Oxford: Clarendon Press, 1970), 13.

to formulate a thoroughly secularized and autonomous version of humanism.

As we shall see in the following chapter, such a humanistic appropriation of empirical science is sometimes presented as an alignment of it within humanism and is referred to as scientific naturalism. This seeks to portray the development of empirical science as progressively achieving an understanding that human subjectivity, conceived as the revealing principle of all meaning and value, is the purpose and goal of all cosmic development.

However, let us first consider a more basic evaluation of the radical significance of empirical science. The approach of scientism claims that it is simply empirical science itself that provides the only reliable access to the ultimate meaning and value of being in general and of human existence in particular, rather than some endeavor to view such science instrumentally as the cognitive procedure to be followed within a broader, more humanistic account.

Two

SCIENTISM AND SCIENTIFIC NATURALISM

I use the term "scientism" to describe the view that, insofar as the ultimate meaning and value of being in general and of human existence in particular can be reliably known, it is exclusively through reliance upon the method and achievements of empirical science and the exploitation of its remarkable technological possibilities. Scientism, in this sense, adopts empirical science as the key to understanding all aspects of human culture, which include its systems of representation, of standards, of expression, and of action. Let us see how such a view might be described, first as a generalized feature of contemporary experience and then as constituting the ultimate philosophical *rationale* of all meaning and value.[1] Later I will consider scientific naturalism, which also portrays empirical science as providing the ultimate context and foundation of all reliable meaning and value, although it involves a somewhat less reductionist perspective than scientism and emphasizes the irreducibility of mind or purpose in nature.

1. I have previously discussed the cultural impact of science and technology in my article "The Arts Degree in an Age of Science and Technology," *The Crane Bag* 7, no. 2 (1983): 33–40. The present discussion is also greatly indebted to Jean Ladriere, *Les enjeux de la rationalité: Le défi de la science et de la technologie aux cultures* (Paris: Aubier-Montaigne, 1977).

Science, Technology, and Contemporary Experience

Modern empirical science and technology differ from more traditional conceptions of scientific knowledge by virtue of their greater dependence on action rather than on contemplative speculation. The modern scientific approach is essentially a matter of reasoning associated with experimentation. Starting from the observation of some puzzling empirical phenomenon, it proceeds to the formulation of an explanatory hypothesis. This hypothesis is formulated as far as possible by means of a mathematical representation of an idealized explanatory model. This hypothesis or explanatory model must be such that it can be tested by subsequent instrumental intervention in a system of phenomena or events for purposes of verification.

The crucial role of operations and instruments in modern science elucidates its intimate connection with modern technology. The two activities are certainly not identical. Science is primarily an activity of abstracting or transforming information objectively realized in the form of natural organization into the form of conceptual representation. Technology is a matter of injecting or transforming information in the form of conceptual representation into information in the form of objectively realized organization. Nevertheless, they are increasingly interdependent and interactive. They form a single, integrated, and dynamic complex structure, a unified domain of operation governed by common theoretical and practical considerations.

Modern science and technology thus tend to become integrated into an all-embracing and unified operational network. They can be viewed as constituting an evolving, cumulative, interconnecting blueprint of rationality that defines its objectives autonomously on the basis of its own internal possibilities and absorbs all other considerations within the ambit of its own inherent dynamism. Their evolution is characteristically one of exploiting possibilities or resolving difficulties that arise from an earlier stage of their development. They tend to produce a seemingly autonomous reality transcending nature and human existence, one whose formal structure is delineated by the conceptual structures of science and whose material embodiment is the worldwide network of technological achievement, for example, in the domains of automation, robotics, and information technology.

This autonomous system of science and technology is at once the product of humanity and also extrinsic to it, tending to impose the law of its own astonishing growth upon the whole range of human experience. It profoundly affects the economic, political, informational, and cultural foci of contemporary social life. Let us briefly consider each of these spheres.

It is obvious that science and technology dominate the economic life of contemporary industrialized societies. Their economic imperative of ever greater productivity and growth is made possible in large measure by new developments in science and technology that continually transform their own foundations. Hence the importance, in modern industrial enterprises, of research and development programs, and the premium that developing countries place on attracting such programs.

Likewise, science and technology play an increasingly important role in political life. This is most obvious in the provisions for military defense and aggression. But it is no less true in those areas where politicians seek to promote development to satisfy the material expectations of their electorate. The funding and coordination

of scientific research and technology assume ever greater importance for governments as they seek to exercise their roles in various
areas such as health, education, housing, employment, communi-
cations, the environment, and energy. One hears that such decisions should be "data-driven." Increasingly the role of government
appears to be one of the scientific and technological manipulations
of society itself. This is true of capitalist systems as well as of those
that are explicitly committed to scientific socialism.

On the cultural level, our society's fundamental self-image is
one that increasingly tends to understand itself, evaluate itself,
and represent itself in terms of the resources of science and technology (not to mention through ever-evolving kinds of information technology). Society tends to see itself as the medium of an
expanding and increasingly autonomous network of scientific and
technological achievement. The scientific ideal of rationality that
aspires to a controlled objective understanding of the world exclusively in terms of this world's own verifiable intrinsic resources
is taken to be the ultimate and all-embracing form of rationality.
Other viewpoints of a religious, mythological, philosophical, or
historical nature are regarded rather dismissively. They are seen as
a futile quest for roots that harkens back to an outdated and naïve
view of reality that the objective scientific outlook has transcended.
We are urged to accept as definitive our condition of uprootedness
and to come to terms with the fact that since the advent of modern
science and technology, we are in the era of the controlled artificial reworking of nature—a reworking that may extend even to the
springs of human life itself. We must, within the constraints and
processes of science, adjust to a new kind of technological equi-
librium with our environment. Religious and other intellectual
traditions can be tolerated under a general enlightened ethic of

toleration and under the recognition that these practices can have therapeutic benefits, but only if the practitioners acknowledge that these beliefs or "spiritualities" are purely personal, not expected to affect decision-making in society or even in one's public life (such as at one's place of employment).

This new "scientific" viewpoint affects our attitude towards every sphere of life and culture, such as entertainment, leisure, the arts, and our moral outlook. It is obvious that science and technology have transformed our conception of entertainment and leisure, notably through their impact upon the media of communication and travel. Our incarnate intersubjectivity is increasingly mediated through impersonal technological capabilities. Our interpersonal relationships are increasingly conducted through the instrumental resources of the computer, the iPad, and the smartphone. Although this can be a source of considerable cultural enrichment, allowing an unprecedented access to both information and people, it is an ambiguous development. As Max Scheler perceived early in the last century, "The abundance of agreeable stimuli here literally deadens the function of enjoyment and its cultivation. The surroundings become ever more glaring, noisy, and stimulating—but men's minds become increasingly joyless. Extremely merry things, viewed by extremely sad people, who do not know what to do with them: that is the 'meaning' of our metropolitan 'culture' of entertainment."[2] One might now add extremely merry things posted on social media by extremely sad people in a vain effort to look as extremely merry as all the other people posting on social media.

The impact of science and technology on the arts is hardly less

2. Max Scheler, *Ressentiment*, trans. William W. Holdheim (New York: Schoken Books, 1972), 154.

dramatic, notably in virtue of the new access to form afforded to the architect, the sculptor, the painter, the musician, and the media artist through new synthetic materials, instruments, and tools. They also impact the modes of distribution and reproduction of these forms of art and the mediated relationships between artists and their admirers.

The scientific mentality likewise affects the moral outlook of our age. One can speak of the spirit of modernity that characterizes the world today as animated by a twin ideal of scientific technological rationalization on the one hand and the attainment of liberation, comprising effective equality and freedom, on the other. This complex ideal involves many inherent tensions between its component elements, but its overall dynamic thrust is undeniable. One could say that this complex ideal envisages a new world, a constructed world, constructed in accordance with the exigencies and possibilities of objective autonomous scientific reason, both theoretical and practical. The distinction between technical possibility and an independent objective foundation in human nature as the basis for moral evaluation tends to be eroded. The norms of human action become those suggested by scientific knowledge and the technological manipulation of natural and artificial systems. The development of the possibilities of science and technology assumes the status of an overriding moral imperative and is taken to be the most effective instrument for the attainment of freedom and equality.

This impersonal scientific and operational outlook becomes the model for moral evaluations and dovetails naturally with a utilitarian ethics that makes its moral evaluations in terms of the objectively calculated outcome of actions. The calculating scientific mentality suggests utilitarian criteria to guide autonomous moral decisions and tends towards the rational manipulation of industrial society by experts along the lines of technocratic managerialism. This has resulted in a willingness to perpetuate some dreadful deeds, such as the large-scale destruction of many innocent victims, if the overall outcome is deemed to be of greater overall utility by the experts. While these worst abuses of rational utilitarianism, especially mass slaughter in the twentieth century, have provoked stronger safeguards for individuals in many countries, the tendency towards looking at human persons as replaceable or disposable continues to gain traction in areas like economic life and medicine.

Another way of putting the point about the all-pervasive cultural influence of scientism is to say that the objective constructed world envisaged by science and technology involves a new conception of temporality that tends to undermine traditional culture's conception of temporality. By their natures science and technology, and their associated ethical impulses towards liberation or autonomy, tend to distance themselves from the existential root system of traditional culture and to adopt more detached, impersonal, and critically rational orientations. In this process the representation of time is significantly altered.

Participants in a traditional culture, whose value systems are typically animated by heroic, religious, or cosmogenic narratives, have access, through appropriate celebrations, rituals, or ceremonies, to a sacred time that lies beyond the everyday time of human experience, which includes the chronological past and the foreseeable future. This sacred time can be viewed as primordial, comprising the originating source of ordinary human time and also the revelation of mysterious events yet to come, as in the Christian tradition. This sacred time, this primordial past and unassignable future, confers ultimate meaning on every moment of historical time past, present, and future, and is thereby contemporaneous with everything that happens. It represents a mysterious adventitious dimension of deliverance and transformation, a truth hiddenly animating the course of history but not on the same axis as the chronological past or the future over which we can in some measure exercise control. It is the milieu of a people's historic memory and imagination, and of their sense of ultimate meaning and purpose.

By contrast, modern science and technology and the associated impulse towards autonomy envisage a more self-contained, controlled, and uniform conception of temporality. The future is related to the past along a horizontal time axis by techniques of calculation and scientific prediction. It is a constructed and rationally anticipated time, such as that of consciously projected and measured five-year development plans and of temporally calculated predetermined research projects. The past loses much of its significance, and the future is what is made to arise out of the present. This assignable future generated by action is responsible only to itself and refers only to its own achievements and programs.

This disturbance of the more traditional temporal scheme has a profound cultural impact. It uproots people from a sense of cosmic at-homeness, in terms of which they have interpreted their existence humanistically or religiously, anchored themselves in a sustaining culture, and achieved a sense of ultimate significance for their lives. It deconstructs accepted tradition, assurances, and hopes, and formulates autonomous, unreceived, and unsecured norms of action. It projects one into a disenchanted world increasingly amenable to scientific calculation and control, but echoing only the logos of its own technology. It is a world whose end becomes identified with its own self-regulating means.

The foregoing line of thought would suggest that the world is, or is in the process of becoming, monocultural. We are, the argument goes, in the era of the progressive disintegration of the historical range of localized and distinctive cultures and of these cultures' progressive reintegration into a uniform global culture. This universal global culture is comprehensively animated by the perspective and possibilities of scientific understanding and technological virtuosity—a virtuosity so triumphantly symbolized at the level of information technology by the worldwide web. Universal global culture unfolds naturally under the invisible hand of market-driven forces. It envisages an all-embracing monoculture, one animated by a scientific, technologically inspired, and rather one-dimensional appraisal of human solidarity. It extols the virtues of indifference, equivalence, and productivity but at the expense of insensitivity to the diverse multidimensional profiles of historically different cultures.

Scientism as Ultimate Explanation

The concrete contemporary lived experience of the all-embracing influence of empirical science and technology is supported reflectively by a theoretical endorsement of the ultimate significance of such science. It is endorsed philosophically as providing the fundamental basis of any insight into the ultimate meaning and value of being in general and of human existence in particular. This philosophical viewpoint has, to a large extent, been formulated in the light of the origin and development of the modern scientific revolution associated with remarkable intellectual innovators such as Copernicus (1473–1543), Galileo (1564–1642), Newton (1643–1727), and Darwin (1809–82).

As I indicated earlier, this revolution inaugurated a new conception of scientific knowledge—a less speculative and more practical experimental one. Methodologically it seeks an intrinsic understanding of the material world in terms of itself rather than an extrinsic understanding in terms of a transcendent creator or any other set of spiritual forces. Reliable scientific knowledge of the world, unlike metaphysical speculation, is to be achieved by a technique which is empirical in a twofold sense. Although traditional metaphysics originates in our experience of aspects of the universe, it seeks an understanding of these experienced realities simply by means of rational reflection or speculation. Such understanding is typically attained by showing the conceptual contradiction involved in its denial. It is often formulated in teleological terms that identify the goal or purpose of these objects of experience, and it ultimately accounts for such goals or purposes in terms of their emanation from or creation by God. I will outline with approval an example of such metaphysical reflection in the next chapter.

Modern science, however, by exploring the objects given to us in sense experience, seeks an understanding of them in terms of mathematically modeled hypotheses about their antecedent efficient physical causes. These hypotheses must be formulated in a manner that can be verified or falsified by means of an experimental procedure that redirects the inquiry back to the world of experience. Modern science thereby contains and restricts the circuit of understanding to within the presupposed context of the experienced material world given to us in sense experience. Metaphysical speculation about the necessary and sufficient conditions of this world itself is beyond the scope, aim, and interest of empirical science.

When such empirical science is adopted as the ultimate and exclusive source of genuine knowledge, it becomes a philosophy or ideology. As an ideology, its form of argument is essentially reductionist. What occurs later in time and is more complex is to be explained in terms of what is prior in time and is physically more basic. Ultimately all explanation, particularly of biological and mental phenomena, is ideally to be provided in terms of basic, mathematically formulated, and empirically verifiable laws of physics and chemistry, which describe the elements the material world is composed of and the laws that govern their spatio-temporal behavior. As the geneticist Professor David McConnell remarked, "There is no borderline between the living and the non-living, and none between humans and non-humans."[3] This is a form of reductionist materialism. It assumes that fundamentally any entity is no more than the sum of its physical parts operating basically according to physical laws of motion—whether the entity considered is the solar system, a flower blossoming, an animal fleeing, or Socrates deciding to remain in prison. It totally rejects any teleological explanation of entities in terms of the purposes or goals they might serve. In this respect it endorses the remark of the seventeenth-century thinker Francis Bacon that "inquiry into final causes is sterile and like a virgin consecrated to God produces nothing."[4]

Associated with this rejection of final causes is the rejection or replacement of any notion of "formal cause" considered as a unifying principle specific to an entity as a whole. The laws of physics (such as the laws of gravitational attraction and thermodynamics) and basic laws of chemistry are universally applicable to every entity of our experience. It seems plausible, therefore, to conclude that it is in terms of such laws, and the initial condition and chance

3. David McConnell, "Why Science Has Made Humanism Inevitable" (Address to the Humanist Association of Ireland, Dublin, July 3, 2016), https://www.humanism.ie/2016/06/first-sunday-meeting-july-3-2016/.

4. Francis Bacon, *De Augmentis Scientarum*, Book III.

mutations of the basic physical particles that they govern, that everything, including the diversity that is manifest in reality, must ultimately be understood. What is essential is the ongoing process of matter in motion, obeying universal laws of physics and chemistry. The product of the process, the specific diversity of reality, is, it would seem reasonable to maintain, simply a non-purposeful accidental spin-off of the process. As Thomas Nagel describes it: "Even if no one yet has a workable idea about the details, it is possible to speculate that the appearance of life was the product of chemical processes governed by the laws of physics, and that evolution after that is likewise due to chemical mutations and natural selection that are just super-complex consequences of physical principles."[5]

This universal reductionism can be viewed as a generalization of the principles of Newtonian physics, which were so dramatically successful in charting the motions of the solar system. The application of these principles is extended to all the motions of all bodies in nature, whether animal, vegetable, or mineral. What we take to be the forms of motion specific to particular kinds of things must, it is affirmed, be understood as merely chance perturbations of a more fundamental, comprehensive, uniform, and law-governed motion. Richard Hassing describes the position well:

This extraordinary generalization is accomplished by the remarkable assumption that every body—including yours and mine—is a vast assemblage of tiny particles that interact by mathematically describable forces and move along trajectories just as astronomical bodies by gravitational force. The analogy here proposed is thus that every body is like a solar

---

5. Thomas Nagel, *Mind and Cosmos: Why the Materialist Neo-Darwinian Conception of Nature Is Almost Certainly False* (Oxford: Oxford University Press, 2011), 19.

system writ small, not in the sense that every body *looks* like the solar system but in the sense that the most basic principles are the same.[6]

We must not, it is asserted, be distracted by the superficial evidence of our senses that different things move and act in basically distinctive manners, each according to the particular sort of thing it is, whether it be a flower blossoming, an animal fleeing, or Socrates deciding to remain in prison. Whole things in nature do not act as such but only as the sum of their dynamically independent parts, which act and interact as they do independently of the whole that they constitute.

At the heart of such scientific reductionism is the assumption that any whole is no more than the sum of its parts. To quote Richard Hassing again:

Whatever we want to know about the behavior of the whole is fully answered in terms of the motions and properties of the parts. The whole is *reducible* to the parts in that the activity of the whole is entailed by the motions and properties of the parts without need of any principle specific to the whole as such—like soul—whereby the activity of the whole would determine the parts, in addition to being determined by the parts.[7]

This reductive materialism provides a theoretical foundation for the pre-philosophical and widely experienced monocultural impact of science and technology. It finds explicit philosophical expression in various versions of positivism, such as that developed by Auguste Comte (1795–1857) in the nineteenth century and the logical positivism of the twentieth century.

---

6. Richard Hassing, "Modern Natural Science and the Intelligibility of Being," in *Final Causality in Nature and Human Affairs*, ed. Hassing (Washington, D.C.: The Catholic University of America Press, 1997), 223.

7. Ibid., 218.

The central theme of Comte's positivist philosophy is his famous Law of the Three States. According to this fundamental doctrine, all speculation on every subject of human inquiry must pass successively through three different theoretical states, both in the case of each individual and in the case of the human race as a whole. These states are (1) the theological, (2) the metaphysical, and (3) the positive.

In the positive state,

the mind has given over the vain search for Absolute notions, the origin and destination of the universe, and the causes of phenomena, and applies itself to the study of their laws—that is, their invariable relations of succession and resemblance. Reasoning and observation, duly combined are the means of this knowledge. What is now understood when we speak of an explanation of fact is simply the establishment of a connection between single phenomena and some general facts, the number of which continually diminishes with the progress of science.[8]

The logical positivism of the twentieth century, typified by A. J. Ayer's philosophical bestseller *Language, Truth, and Logic*, maintained that all knowledge claims other than tautologies or empirically verifiable propositions are neither true nor false but strictly speaking meaningless. The simplest, most unified, verifiable physical laws provide the ultimate explanation of everything. It is futile to speculate metaphysically why such laws hold. One simply accepts the empirical evidence that ultimately this is how things are.

Such "scientism," which absolutizes a reductive materialist conception of empirical science, is compatible with neither theistic belief in a divine creator nor any interpretation of humanism

---

8. Auguste Comte, *The Positive Philosophy of Auguste Comte*, trans. and condensed by Harriet Martineau (London: Chapman, 1853), 1:2.

that affirms the absolute priority of human consciousness as the perspective from which all meaning and value must be established and appraised. As I will indicate below when considering scientific naturalism, there have been attempts to envisage empirical science as somehow disclosing a basically teleological process of evolution. It is suggested that this process, although activated and governed exclusively by physical principles, is inherently disposed to facilitate the emergence of humanity as the natural cosmic product for the attainment and continuous development of various levels of objective value, such as aesthetic, social, political, and moral values. Such conceptions envisage some form of humanism as a natural but dependent accompaniment of a primarily scientific conception of ultimate meaning and value. However, it is difficult to reconcile such "purposeful" conceptions of natural science with its own prevailing rejection of any form of teleological thinking.

Notwithstanding the very widespread acceptance of such reductive materialism, it is certainly not the unquestionable response to any inquiry into the ultimate meaning and value of being in general and of human existence in particular. Its truth is neither self-evident nor convincingly demonstrated, and it fails dramatically to provide anything approaching a convincing account of certain important considerations.

The claim that only empirically verifiable propositions are cognitively informative is not itself an empirically verifiable proposition. Undoubtedly it is a view held with great conviction that indeed expresses the prevailing consensus of many in the scientific community. But it is not an empirically verifiable truth. Neither is its associated and more concrete claim that the basic laws of physics and chemistry provide the ultimate explanation of everything that pertains to the spatio-temporal material world of our experience.

35

The remarkable success of empirical science in expanding our knowledge of this world encourages a commitment to such science as the only assured and dependable cognitive resource we have. This claim in itself, however, is just a widely endorsed commitment and not a self-evident or demonstrated truth.

More significantly, the reductionist claim to provide—or at least to anticipate—a comprehensive quantitative understanding of the world's activity simply in terms of mathematically formulated physical laws that describe the movement of basic material particles fails to take into account certain important and undeniable considerations. These include the inability of such a claim to provide a convincing account of the origin of life and, more fundamentally, an account of the emergence of rational beings or persons. Reductionist materialism claims that life and mind, which subsist in a material context, must be ultimately and fully explicable, like everything else, in terms of the basic laws of physics and chemistry. But it does not demonstrate how this is so. It is a hope or an assumption rather than a scientifically verified hypothesis.

The origin of life is a hotly debated topic. The immense amount of internally controlling sequential information, as distinct from externally imposed order, that is required for the achievement of even a single living cell poses a genuine objection to the prevailing scientific assumption about the origin of life. This assumption states that all life and biological processes are merely the chance outcomes of exclusively physicochemical systems that are enabled by some fortuitous sequence of events analogous to the natural selection by replication and mutation that is characteristic of already living entities. Nevertheless, this momentous assumption, however attractive to a reductionist viewpoint, has not been verified, and observations about the structural complexity of even a single living cell do not suggest that its verification is imminent or likely. As Professor Stuart Kaufmann put it more bluntly, "Anyone who tells you that he or she knows how life started on earth some 3.45 billion years ago is a fool or a knave. Nobody knows."[9]

The difficulty concerning the prevailing scientific assumption about the initial origin of life is increased rather than lessened by a retrospective consideration of it from the perspective of higher forms of life such as consciousness and the exercise of theoretical and practical reason. For these higher forms of life are clearly less consistent with a purely reductionist interpretation of the whole natural order exclusively in terms of physical science. Such reductionism seeks to determine the basic physical components of everything and to show how they might combine to explain the organic complexity and accompanying levels of consciousness and rational life that we observe.

Consciousness and rational life are features of living bodies with nervous systems, living bodies and systems that are part of the physical world. These conscious and intelligent bodies are fundamentally composed of the same physical elements as everything else in nature. According to reductionist materialism, then, they should be fully describable by the same laws of physics and chemistry that govern the rest of the physical world, although admittedly involving greater complexity.

However, the consciousness evidenced in animal activity—for example, the interrogative regard of one's dog anticipating its daily walk—already conveys the distinct impression of a form of subjectivity that transcends the scope of purely physical or chemical explanation. Reductionists tend to identify such phenomena with

9. Stuart Kaufmann, *At Home in the Universe* (London: Viking Press, 1995), 31.

various behavioral dispositions. In other words, the various indications of animal consciousness are reduced to their externally observable behavioral manifestations, which are then interpreted as simply exotic aspects of the physical world, a world that evolved accidentally and cumulatively by random processes of mutation and duplication.

But such an account is incomplete and leaves out, or abstracts from, the essential features of animal consciousness—namely, the animal's inner awareness or subjective viewpoint from which it experiences its environment and which finds expression in the external behavioral manifestations that reductionists fasten upon as the whole story. From our own basic, instinctual, emotional, and sensible experiences, we are empathically aware that these observable organic and behavioral phenomena are expressions of a distinctively subjective, internal, and conscious perspective or point of view that is irreducible to exclusively external third-person objective description and explanation.

Such observations are even more obvious and compelling when one considers the characteristically rational activities of our human existence. As Thomas Nagel remarks, "Just as consciousness cannot be explained as a mere extension or complication of physical evolution, so reason cannot be explained as a mere extension or complication of consciousness. To explain our rationality will require something in addition to what is needed to explain our consciousness and its evidently adaptive forms, something at a different level."[10]

Since at least the time of Aristotle, it has been generally agreed that a human being is most appropriately described as a rational animal. The challenge is to unfold this insight in a way that main-

10. Nagel, *Mind and Cosmos*, 81–82.

tains the unity and paradoxical complexity of such being. This challenge has been addressed in various ways. There have been attempts to absolutize the "animal" component and interpret the rational component reductively from the perspective of an exclusively materialist conception of the human condition. Likewise, there have been attempts to absolutize the "rational" aspect and explain away the animal component by way of some version of philosophical idealism. Alternatively, there is the attempt to explain away by separation the composite unity of both components. Such an approach is found in various versions of philosophical dualism. These versions claim that there are two radically distinct but somehow interacting beings involved in human existence: a material being and a rational or spiritual being. This claim has been described as viewing a human being as a ghost in a machine!

Avoiding such distractions, I wish to concentrate on our experiential evidence that a human person is one being, a psychophysical unity simultaneously and substantially both material and intelligent. However, although each intelligent human being is thus intimately dependent for her reality upon her incarnation in a conscious organic material medium, her characteristic rational activity exceeds or transcends the resources of this material context.

At the heart of this characteristically rational activity is our ability to obtain objective truth—the ability to know how things are and how we should act. We claim access to truths that are obtained independently of our immediate experience, instincts, emotions, desires, or prejudices. We even claim the capacity to make scientific statements about how the world was prior to any human existence or experience and how it would be when there might no longer be any such existence or experience. In virtue of our intelligence, we transcend the pragmatic immediacy of our sensory involvement in the world and exercise the ability to attain detached objective truth of both a theoretical and a practical nature. We really know, admittedly fallibly and to a limited extent, what truly and objectively is the case and what it is right to do.

Through our rational activity, we have access to objective truths in domains such as logic, mathematics, empirical science, and philosophy. We also devise and rely upon highly sophisticated technology that depends upon our possession of such truths. And rather than acting simply according to immediately perceived needs or wants, we discern and accept reasons for action that motivate us because they represent objective moral requirements.[11] Influenced by what the poet Seamus Heaney calls "the gravitational pull of the actual," we can even occasionally create works of great beauty that disclose further compelling truth about reality.[12]

All such activity surpasses what might be deduced from our scientific knowledge of our physical and chemical composition. Indeed, upon reflection, such scientific knowledge manifests itself operationally, if not axiomatically, as involving more than the physical and chemical operation of the physical particles that reductionist materialism declares to be the ultimate and exclusive source of everything. In other words, such an exercise of intelligence, by its very nature and operation, exceeds and thereby refutes the claim that everything is reducible to matter in motion. The mental activity by which reductive materialism comes to be formulated and affirmed refutes reductive materialism itself, much in the same way that providing an argument that questions the reliability of logical reasoning is self-defeating since any such argument must use logical reasoning and thereby presuppose its reliability. Thought

11. Nagel, *The Possibility of Altruism*, 13.

12. Seamus Heaney, *The Redress of Poetry* (London: Faber and Faber, 1995), 3.

and rational argument cannot be adequately reformulated in terms of electrochemical neural events. Such events simply occur: they cannot engage in rational discourse and cannot be right or wrong, valid or invalid.

Human intelligence has undoubtedly developed and emerged subsequent to and dependent upon its undeniably material antecedents. Moreover, its activity requires and operates dependently upon the previously evolved realization of a living organism with a complex central nervous system and a highly developed brain. However, this does not justify a *post hoc propter hoc* type of explanation of intelligence in terms of its historically prior preconditions. Its distinctive activity involves more than physics, chemistry, molecular biology, and neurophysiology can reveal about the nature and development of these necessary material preconditions.

Such disciplines disclose important scientific truths about these preconditions of human intelligence. But they do not explain the actualization and exercise of this intelligence and its ability to attain, inter alia, autonomous necessary truths of logic, objective scientific truths about the natural world, and moral truths about appropriate human action. This actualization and exercise of human intelligence attains a radically new level of reality utterly irreducible to its material medium.

Precisely as beings, different individuals constitute an analogical hierarchy, a more and less of perfection. Thus, while a stone is limited to an exclusively material mode of being—one comprehensible in terms of physics and chemistry—a person transcends such limitation and enjoys an essentially more comprehensive and perfect mode of being. Here we speak of biological and cognitive structures that, like an intelligible text in respect to its component ink molecules (but unlike a bicycle in respect to its parts), are neither reducible to nor predictable from the physicophysical components in which they subsist.

Human beings belong to and are integrated with the whole physical universe.[13] They are part of it, part of the same natural system that includes both living and inanimate material things. Yet human beings also exceed or transcend the intrinsic capacities and physicochemical interactions of their microparts. They do so chiefly in virtue of their more-than-material "spiritual" or rational active ability to attain objective knowledge, to form intentions, and to make reflective decisions. Such "spiritual" intelligent activity certainly exercises causal activity on its environment. However, it is a distinctive kind of activity, one that operates rationally by way of intentional meaning and purposeful decisions rather than simply by mechanical propulsion or chemical interaction of physical components (although obviously such decisions presuppose and can affect such phenomena). Notwithstanding the universal validity of Newtonian mechanics, Socrates can decide to stay put in prison (with all the physical implications) instead of making a run for it as his friends implored.

Causation according to meaning by way of intelligent insight and intentional decision is an activity operating at an entirely different level from physical causation, which operates mechanically and is oblivious to consciousness of what is meaningful or nonsensical. Thus, an adding machine cannot even add, and a computer does not know what it is computing. (The contrast is somewhat like the difference between a toaster toasting a piece of bread and one's self toasting the bread at a fire!) Until a genuinely cognitive computer is constructed (if ever), it is reasonable to maintain that the

13. James Ross, "Christians Get the Best of Evolution," in *Evolution and Creation*, ed. Ernan McMullin, 223–51 (Notre Dame, Ind.: Notre Dame University Press, 1985).

"spiritual" domain in which human beings participate is a distinct level of reality and one that is required for intelligent life.[14] It is as thus pertaining to a "spiritual" level of reality, notwithstanding their belonging within the physical universe, that human beings as intelligent rational agents can be said to be emergent vis-à-vis their material microparts. They exist as agents who can operate in the realm of logical implication that is incommensurable with the realm of physical causality. They exist as body-subject, not merely as body-object.

This emergence of human beings as intelligent rational agents can be viewed as a coming-into-play and conscious exercise of a level of principles of reason or intelligence, describable in terms of laws of thought and logic. Such laws include the principle of contradiction, which affirms that "contradictory statements cannot both be true at the same time," and the principle of material implication, which affirms that "a true statement cannot validly imply a false one." The conscious exercise of such principles enables the formulation of rational argument, which is a different order of activity than the law-like physical interaction of two colliding billiard balls.

Such actively exercised principles and the laws that describe their activity are quite distinct from the principles governing physical activity, describable in terms of laws of physics and chemistry. This distinction implies a view of the natural order, which includes human beings, as comprising a hierarchy of levels of reality, some of which become operative only at an appropriate level of physical complexity. All of this indicates a nonexclusively materialist conception of evolution. Rational human beings can emerge or come to exist as a completely new and irreducible "whole" when a par-

14. Ibid., 226.

ticular stage of material development or evolution is attained. This complex stage of material development functions as the adequate material medium in which principles of rational or intelligent being can activate and operate as the distinctive features of the natural order that they are. Such principles of intelligent human activity are described in terms of laws of logical reasoning, laws of scientific inquiry, and laws or general maxims for moral action.

The new emergent "whole" or "totality" is not an accidental construction caused by a contrived assembly of its parts into a whole, such as that of a sandcastle or a bicycle. The new human reality, emergent as an actualized possibility in a suitably disposed material medium, is not caused or produced by its constituent material parts and their arrangement and interaction. Rather, it is in virtue of the new and irreducible human form or nature that these constituent material parts are caused to be the specifically human parts of a newly emerged whole entity. Thus, as Hegel perceptively remarks:

The limbs and organs, for instance, of an organic body are not merely parts of it: it is only in their unity that they are what they are, and they are unquestionably affected by this unity, as they also in turn affect it. The limbs and organs become parts, only when they pass under the hands of the anatomist, whose occupation, be it remembered, is not with the living body but with the corpse. Not that such analysis is illegitimate: we only mean that the external and mechanical relation of whole and parts is not sufficient for us, if we want to study organic life in its truth.[15]

And some centuries earlier, Aquinas, adopting Aristotle's hylomorphic theory remarked:

15. G. F. Hegel, *Encyclopaedia Logic*, trans. William Wallace (Oxford: Oxford University Press, 1892), par. 135.

Now the substantial form perfects not only the whole, but each part of the whole. A form of the whole which does not give existence to each part of the body, is a form consisting in composition and order, such as the form of a house, and such a form is accidental. But the soul is a substantial form, and therefore it must be the form and the act, not only of the whole, but also of each part.[16]

That a human being, emerging as a new whole into effective and active existence, is capable of both theoretical and practical reasoning when the human body in which he subsists has developed or evolved an appropriate nervous system and brain is indeed an astonishing phenomenon. We can empathize with Aristotle's wonder nearly two and a half thousand years ago when he remarked: "At what moment, and in what manner, do these creatures which have this principle of Reason acquire their share in it and where does it come from? This is a very difficult problem. . . . It remains then that Reason alone enters in as an additional factor, from outside, and that it alone is divine, because physical activity has nothing whatsoever to do with the activity of Reason."[17]

I think that he would have understood and accepted the claim that, although rational human beings can only begin to exist as necessarily subsistent in a material bodily medium (which is an evolved complex system of organic molecules), precisely as rational or intelligent human beings they are radically emergent and not deducible simply from this material medium. As James Ross remarks, "We have being materially but are not just material things."[18] (We shall see in a later chapter how this key concept of "emergence" also

16. Thomas Aquinas, *Summa theologiae*, trans. English Dominicans (London: Eyre and Spottiswoode, 1964–74) I, q. 76, art. 8.

17. Aristotle, *Generation of Animals*, trans. A. L. Peck, (Cambridge, Mass.: Harvard University Press, 1942), 736b.

18. Ross, "Christians Get the Best of Evolution," 236.

plays a central role in elucidating the most remarkable characteristic of our human reality, namely, our capacity to love.)

The laws that describe what makes possible and what governs the effective realization of intelligent life are distinct and underivable from the laws of physics, even though intelligent human life implies material being and therefore the laws of physics. The structure of intelligent human life cannot be derived from the structure of material being even though it implies or presupposes it.

Further, one must distinguish between our human epistemological formulation of various laws that describe the actions of things and the corresponding objective ontological activity itself, which is really operative at various levels of being—in other words, the distinction between the cognitive description of real activity and the objectively real activity itself, which such cognitive descriptions designate. Our knowledge of the objective validity of the laws of physics and chemistry is itself already an exercise of the higher activity characteristic of intelligent life. What such knowledge denotes is understood to be physical activity, which is antecedent to and different from the nature and activity of the human intelligence that affirms it and that is underivable from it.

Becoming an intelligent human being is not just another accidental way of changing as a material being, like the way in which becoming red is an accidental way of changing as a tomato. Although human life exists in a material medium, the exercise of this intelligent life reveals it as operating at a higher or fuller level of being than an exclusively material being. The emergent intelligent being has a form or way of being disparate and inaccessible from that of its material components.

Accepting the incommensurability of an appropriate account of rational human life with an exclusively materialist conception of everything certainly seems incompatible with a reductionist conception of empirical science. Such a conception seeks to explain the entire natural order, including consciousness and mind, ultimately and exclusively in terms of the basic laws of physics and chemistry. One could say that it seeks to explain first-person phenomena exclusively in third-person terms.

There is, however, another empirical science-based approach that argues in a less reductionist way, although it still sees empirical science, understood broadly, as providing the only reliable approach to meaning and value. To distinguish it from the strict reductionism of scientism, we will refer to it as scientific naturalism. Scientific naturalism acknowledges the distinctive reality of each of the various levels or degrees of being that characterize the natural world, and it seeks to provide a nonreductive account of this analogical and ontological diversity of the natural order while remaining within the methodological limits of empirical science. It recognizes that the various irreducible levels of reality must be considered by means of various irreducible levels of empirical scientific inquiry, such as genetics, biology, neurology, psychology, anthropology, sociology, and political science as well as the basic sciences, physics and chemistry. I outline a brief account of such an approach below.

Scientific Naturalism

Scientific naturalism presents itself as an empirically controlled scientific attempt to understand the evolving development of the natural order as somehow intrinsically oriented to the realization and increasingly more diversified expression of objective meaning and value. It is guided by what it claims to be an empirically verifiable hypothesis that the natural order embodies an inherent cosmic blueprint or goal. This blueprint or goal predetermines how the initial systematic arrangement of physical particles is disposed and enabled to evolve in a regulated but not inescapably deterministic manner to accomplish the progressive realization and development of a domain of meaning and value. This perspective has a closer affinity to humanism than to a strictly reductionist scientism.

Scientific naturalism is a conception that involves a teleological view of the historical development of the natural order. It sees this historical development as proceeding, from its origin in the initial "big bang," and developing as drawn towards an outcome or goal, through evolving structures of increasing complexity, to the existence of life, consciousness, and a level of human rationality that can recognize and promote a domain of meaning and value. Such an approach rejects the prevailing commitment to reductive materialism only characterized by chance mutations and subsequent natural selection. It affirms the reality of purposefulness in the temporal unfolding of nature. This approach, excluding any appeal to an external designer, claims that the natural order contains the capacity to attain its natural intrinsic goal exclusively within its own resources. It is an imaginative conception of the ultimate meaning and value of everything, one that claims that the world is intrinsically ordered to come to know itself and to promote the reality of objective values through the scientific and moral achievement of its highest dimension and attainment, namely, humanity.

Thomas Nagel provides a stimulating account of such an approach in his above-mentioned book *Mind and Cosmos*. He maintains that if one accepts antireductionist arguments, one is rationally required to seek an alternative unified conception of the natural order. It is intellectually unsatisfactory to simply maintain that, although the reductionist materialism characteristic of scientism is unsatisfactory, there is no comprehensive unified natural order in which everything hangs together—just disconnected forms and levels of intelligibility and understanding. Nagel argues that if one is convinced of the inadequacy of reductionist materialism (which believes that everything, including consciousness, intentionality, meaning, decision, and value, can be accounted for in terms of physical science), one must seek an alternative, comprehensive, and unified account of the entire natural order that accords distinctive significance to such phenomena. "The possibility opens up of a pervasive conception of the natural order very different from materialism—one that makes mind central, rather than a side effect of physical law. . . . A genuine alternative to the reductionist program would require an account of how mind and everything that goes with it is inherent in the universe"[19]

One is led to envisage a unified conception of the natural order that is such that mind is doubly related to it. "Nature is such as to give rise to conscious beings with minds; and it is such as to be comprehensible to such beings. . . . And these are fundamental features of the universe, not byproducts of contingent developments whose true explanation is given in terms that do not make reference to mind."[20]

In effect, what Nagel envisages is a normative way of understanding a unified natural order that includes the mental as an irreducible component. However, this account remains strictly secular and scientific and confines itself simply to providing a theory of the immanent and intrinsic order of nature.

19. Nagel, *Mind and Cosmos*, 15.
20. Ibid., 17.

49

Such an understanding of the natural order is not susceptible to a reductionist explanation. Nagel suggests, somewhat tentatively, that it yields an alternative explanation in terms of a natural teleology that envisages the cosmos as inherently disposed to the historical emergence of life, consciousness, and theoretical and practical reason.

This natural teleological explanation would claim that, besides the timeless and basic (but not entirely deterministic) natural features of the universe (describable by the quantitative laws of physics that underlie efficient causation), there are other natural features of the universe describable in terms of principles or laws that ensure that things develop over time on a path of increasing complexity, which leads naturally to certain outcomes such as conscious and value-affirming rational organisms.[21] Such a teleological conception of the evolution of the cosmos is supported by our recognition of the reality of theoretical and practical values that provide us with objective reasons to guide and control our affirmations, our decisions, and our conduct.

This idea of teleology implies the reality of values towards which animate, conscious and, in particular, rational beings tend, as towards a good that is their fulfillment or goal. The recognition by rational human beings of such objective values provides not only theoretical knowledge but also objective reasons for action. We can aim consciously at our own fulfillment or good and indeed at whatever is intrinsically good. The active pursuit of value gives our lives purpose. As Nagel puts it, "On a teleological account, the existence of value is not an accident, because that is part of the explanation of why there is such a thing as life, with all its possibilities of development and variation. In brief, value is not just an accidental side

21. Ibid., 47–53.

effect of life; rather there is life because life is a necessary condition of value."[22]

Besides the value-free operation of the physical and chemical features of the universe, there is a cosmic predisposition to an evolved form of life and the value associated with it. A remarkable feature of teleology is that the complex organization of an evolved form of life, an organization that enables the realization and recognition of value, is to be explained not simply in terms of antecedent physical causes but also in terms of the very value that the organization accomplishes.

There are thus at least two very different "scientific" approaches to the question of meaning and value. The most influential, scientism, is in the form of a reductive materialism that aspires to understand everything ultimately in terms of the basic laws of physics. The other—scientific naturalism, which affirms various irreducible levels of reality and especially the irreducible reality of the mind—proposes a teleological account of reality in terms of a historical tendency of the universe to evolve to a realization and recognition of value.

Although these approaches are very different, they share the same basic perspective. Both seek the basis of all meaning and value exclusively in terms of the intrinsic resources of the natural world of our experience. Both preclude any appeal to an external explanation such as the existence of a provident God. As the British philosopher Anthony Flew remarked some time before his subsequent "conversion" to theism, "The presumption, defeasible of course by adverse arguments, must be that all qualities observed in things belong by natural right to those things themselves and hence that whatever characteristics we think ourselves able to discern in

22. Ibid., 122–23.

the universe as a whole are the underivative characteristics of the universe itself. This is, for us, atheism."[23]

This discussion of humanism, scientism, and scientific naturalism describes the contemporary context of serious and influential thought from which to initiate a discussion of an alternative response to the question of ultimate meaning and value—the theistic response. I must declare again that it is the one that I am personally persuaded makes most (though not ineluctable) sense. As theism is the response I argue for from personal conviction, I will devote most attention to it and will consider it from various aspects. If I am successful in this endeavor, the less exhaustive (but hopefully fair) impersonal presentations that I have offered of humanism, scientism, and scientific naturalism will to some extent be justified.

A realist theory of knowledge, which affirms the objective reality of cosmic development and intelligibility as obtaining independently of our conscious apprehension of it, poses a problem for the humanist claim that our conscious subjectivity is the ultimate source of all meaning and value. The irreducibly first-person claims of human subjectivity pose a problem for "scientistic" reductive materialism. A teleologically elaborated conception of empirical science, such as that proposed by scientific naturalism and postulated as providing the ultimate and necessary basis of all meaning and value, faces the difficulty that such a conception is not a self-evidently sufficient explanation. One can ask in what sense, if any, this "necessary" teleological explanation of the meaning and value disclosed by the natural world itself is a rational necessity rather than an ultimately inexplicable brute fact. Such explanation may articulate more effectively than strictly reductionist materialism the necessary enabling intrinsic conditions of the analogically

23. Antony Flew, *God and Philosophy* (London: Hutchinson, 1966), 3.30.

diversified existence of the natural world as we experience it. But it does not provide or explain the necessity of the existence of these necessary enabling intrinsic conditions themselves. Thus John Haldane remarks: "If the necessary conditions of our existence did not obtain, we would not exist, and if the necessary conditions of the necessary conditions of our existence had not obtained, then neither we nor many other aspects and elements of the present universe would have been.... Cosmic regularity makes our existence possible; the underlying issue concerns the enabling conditions of this order itself."[24]

Such considerations relating to the unresolved objections to or difficulties associated with humanism, scientism, and scientific naturalism direct attention to the theistic response on the issue of the ultimate meaning of being in general and of human existence in particular. This is not to imply that a defense of theism is problem-free plain sailing. For example, one has only to advert to the obdurate nature of the problem of evil in a world created by an infinitely good God. But let us now proceed to a consideration of how a case for theism as the ultimate source of all meaning and value might be developed.

24. John Haldane, "Philosophy Lives," *First Things* 209 (January 2011): 45.

Three

PHILOSOPHICAL THEISM AND
RELIGIOUS BELIEF

One of the challenges that the development of a plausible account of theism faces today is the widespread acceptance and influence of the alternative accounts of the ultimate source of meaning and value—namely, humanism, scientism, and scientific naturalism. This difficulty is accentuated by the fact that, in many respects, the development and acceptance of each of these alternatives has involved an explicit repudiation of a previously prevailing theistic conviction as unconvincing, unnecessary, or even humanly alienating.

The humanist affirmation of the absolute and irreducible primacy of human subjectivity as the ultimate source of meaning and value disputes as contrary to its guiding inspiration any attempted interpretation of this subjectivity as deriving from and radically dependent upon a divine creator. Similarly, the scientist's affirmation of the empirical scientific method as the ultimate source of knowledge, which locates the context of all reliable meaning and value within the intrinsic resources of the natural world that we experience, also involves a rejection of any external divine cause or explanation. A contemporary defense of theism must take into account these characteristically post-theistic alternatives to the question of ultimate meaning and value.

The term "theism" has various shades of meaning. We can adopt, at least provisionally, the *Encyclopedia Britannica* definition: "Theism is the view that all limited or finite things are dependent in some way or other on one supreme or ultimate reality of which one may also speak in personal terms."[1] More concretely, theism is the view that the entire universe is dependent for its being, its continued existence, and its activity upon the free benevolent act of a provident and infinitely perfect creator.

Theism is intimately related to, though not quite synonymous with, religious faith and belief. Most theists are religious believers. However, one might conceivably accept a theoretical theistic argument but decline its practical religious implications. Indeed, a feature of contemporary atheism is often its rejection, in the name of human autonomy, of the self-involving religious commitment that theism is understood to imply. Even if one does not proclaim a Luciferian "Non Serviam," one might accept Sartre's less dramatic humanistic observation: "What have I to do with you or you with me? We shall glide past each other, like ships in a river, without touching. You are God and I am free: each of us is alone, and our anguish is akin."[2]

Nevertheless, theism as a specific form of philosophical inquiry and affirmation has evolved historically within a context of monotheistic religious belief (for example, Judeo-Christian belief). Such belief is typically presented as involving an affirmation of God conceived as provident creator of the world rather than as just its supreme intrinsic dimension, as Greek philosophers thought. However, this theistic affirmation is usually maintained as pri-

1. Lewis, Hywel David. "Theism." In *Encyclopedia Britannica*. Article published July 26, 1999; last modified April 15, 2019. https://www.britannica.com/topic/theism.

2. Jean-Paul Sartre, *The Flies*, trans. Stuart Gilbert (New York: Knopf, 1947), 158.

marily a pre-philosophical faith-grounded theological affirmation rather than as a philosophically argued conclusion. Among various theological elaborations of such religious faith in God, there are very different conceptions of the role or even the possibility of strictly philosophical discussion and argument about the existence and nature of God. This difference is illustrated by the difference in relative value traditionally accorded by Protestant and Catholic theologians to the role of natural human reason vis-à-vis divine grace in their accounts of Christian religious faith.

In general, Catholic theologians have traditionally affirmed that a distinct and positive role is to be ascribed to human reason in considering questions concerning the existence and nature of God. On the other hand, Protestant theologians in the tradition of Martin Luther tend to minimize the significance of the independent role of human reason and indeed sometimes see it as constituting an obstacle rather than a help.[3] The contrasting positions are perspicuously illustrated by Karl Barth in the Protestant tradition and Thomas Aquinas in the Catholic.

According to Barth, dependable knowledge about God is attained not through the independent exercise of our natural reason but only through faith in his self-revelation to us. The attainment of this faith has nothing to do with natural human knowledge. It is the work of God's grace alone, an act of God operating in human consciousness, which enables one to recognize one's sinful nature and to acknowledge Jesus Christ as Savior and Redeemer. The idea that the arguments of natural theology have any role to play as a rational presupposition of the attainment of religious faith is an

---

3. Against these general tendencies, it should be said that some of the most vigorous philosophical defenders of the existence of God in recent decades are Protestants (e.g., philosopher Alvin Plantinga of the University of Notre Dame, a member of the Reformed tradition that owes more to John Calvin than to Luther).

illusion, and a dangerous one at that. "Moreover, all the articles of our Christian belief are, when considered rationally, just as impossible, mendacious and preposterous. Faith, however, is completely abreast of the situation. It grips reason by the throat and strangles the beast."[4] Alleged naturally acquired knowledge of God is not part of the solution to the challenge to provide a reliable account of faith. It is part of the problem. For all reliance on simply our natural intelligence to enlighten us, even in a preliminary way, about the existence and nature of God can result only in idolatry.

Clearly, Barth's theology of faith has no role for the traditional arguments of natural theology, such as the five proofs for the existence of God proposed by Aquinas. Barth explicitly rejected the affirmation of the First Vatican Council that "God, the beginning and end of all things, may be certainly known by the natural light of human reason, by means of created things."[5]

Aquinas, in contrast with Barth, attributes considerable importance to natural reason in developing an account of religious faith. However, although this is undoubtedly true, it needs to be understood in a rather qualified sense. In the first place, according to Aquinas we have no natural knowledge of the self-evident nature of God's existence and no direct awareness of his existence. "This arises from the weakness of our intellect which cannot behold God Himself except through His effects and which is thus led to know His existence through reasoning."[6] Secondly, Aquinas is as insistent as Barth in maintaining that theology, unlike the natu-

4. Karl Barth, *The Epistle to the Romans*, trans. Edwyn C. Hosykns (Oxford: Oxford University Press, 1933), 143–44.

5. Vatican Council I, Dogmatic Constitution *Dei Filius* II (April 24, 1870).

6. Thomas Aquinas, *Summa contra Gentiles: On the Truth of the Catholic Faith*, trans. Anton Pegis, J. F. Anderson, V. J. Bourke, and C. J. O'Neill (New York: Doubleday, 1955–57) I, ch. 11.

ral knowledge attained in philosophy, originates and proceeds, as from a first principle, from faith in God and in what he has revealed to us about himself and about our relationship to him.

Thirdly, for Aquinas the light of faith, the *lumen fidei*, provides the believer with much greater and more perfect knowledge of God than is accessible to natural reason.[7] However, for him, this does not signify that the natural reason of the believer is raised by faith to a new kind or level of intellectual insight. The light of the believer's faith does not give her intellectual access to a new and superior meaning of the supernatural truths proposed to faith—a meaning which is inaccessible to the understanding of the unbeliever. The meaning, though not the truth, of articles of faith is indeed fully accessible to natural human understanding—in the same sense to the reason of the unbeliever as to that of the believer. Inasmuch as it relates only to human intelligence, faith does not yet truly unite us to God. "For faith is about what is absent, not about what is present. However, God is made affectively present when by his will the believer assents to God."[8]

This affective presence of God engendered by the graced will's loving movement to embrace what is proposed to faith is not a matter of attaining new or additional knowledge about the divine object of faith. It is a matter of us being enabled to relate *ourselves* more intimately, personally, and lovingly to what is already known intellectually as proposed to faith. As Georges Van Riet remarks:

The role in faith of the *lumen fidei* is not to enable us to discover a new *meaning* in the statements of faith, but rather to orient us to God in his reality. It makes us feel or "grasp affectively" that in these statements it is God who reveals himself. Consequently, in virtue of this affective grasp

7. Aquinas, *Summa theologiae* I, q. 12, art. 13.

8. Aquinas, *Summa contra Gentiles* III, ch. 40.

it enables us to adhere intellectually (with complete certitude, based on the authority of God, the first Truth) to the truth of these non-evident statements.[9]

The foregoing considerations indicate that, contrary to what is sometimes suggested, Aquinas had a rather measured and qualified view of the role of the natural human intellect in an appropriate account of the faith of the believer. The intellect does not grasp intuitively the truth of what it affirms by faith. This truth is achieved through the graced movement of the will adhering lovingly to what is proposed to us to believe.

Nevertheless, it remains true that Aquinas places great confidence in the role of human reason in the development of his theology. A powerful motivation of his insistence upon the competence and importance of natural reason and metaphysical argument within theology is his conviction that the light of faith cannot be at odds with human reason. Faith and reason, he insists, are necessarily compatible with each other. Faith, considered as a light or grace that enables us to adhere freely to divine revelation, can be such a light only because we are able to see and understand what it proposes. Even though it is God who enables the faith of the believer by grace, he does so through a gracious determination and enabling of our natural ability of free will to lovingly assent to what our intellect understands but cannot affirm by itself. Some truths about God are attainable only through faith in his gracious revelation, while other truths about God are available through rational reflection on his creation. They cannot contradict one another for they each derive ultimately from God, the unique source of all truth.

Hence, for Aquinas, there are truths such as the existence of

9. Georges Van Riet, *Philosophie et religion* (Paris: Editions Beatrice Nauwelaerts, 1970), 77. My translation.

God that, strictly speaking, are not articles of faith since they are accessible to natural reason. Such truths, however, are for the most part held on faith since their attainment by reason is precarious and usually only available in circumstances in which ability and leisure obtain to devote time to the serious philosophical inquiry involved.

The feature of this theological account of the relationship between faith and reason that contrasts most obviously with Barth's account is Aquinas's claim that some of the truths revealed about God are accessible to natural reason. These are the metaphysical truths featured in natural theology (so abhorrent to Barth), which claim to provide dependable knowledge, by way of our natural intelligence alone, about the existence and attributes of God, such as his goodness, unity, and omniscience. Once successfully attained through natural theology, these naturally knowable truths of faith are known and therefore no longer simply believed, unlike the indemonstrable truths of faith such as the doctrines of the Trinity and the Incarnation, which are utterly beyond the range of our natural intelligence.

In contemporary theism, this rather clear-cut distinction between theological approaches that include a role for the *a posteriori*, objective, metaphysical arguments of natural theology and those that exclude them tends to be sidelined. There is an expanding consensus, one that includes Catholic as well as Protestant theologians and philosophers, that such traditional metaphysical arguments about the existence and nature of God are at best noncompelling and, more significantly, inappropriate and even misleading. A different role for philosophy in its relation to religious belief is proposed by proponents of both phenomenology and linguistic philosophy.

In due course, I will offer some critical observations about this fashionable repudiation of the metaphysical reasoning characteristic of traditional natural theology. However, before these reflections I must describe the alternative role actually ascribed to philosophy in defense of theism by both phenomenology and linguistic philosophy.

Phenomenology and linguistic philosophy argue that the philosophical appraisal of religious belief should not be conducted by way of some form of abstract objective metaphysical reasoning about puzzling features of the material world. Rather, such philosophical appraisal should be by way of reflective description and appraisal of the insights and disclosures that religious experience and belief reveal to our consciousness as authentic and irreducible human phenomena. Let us consider this form of philosophy of religion, which is common to approaches in both continental phenomenology and Anglo-American linguistic philosophy. One approach seeks to develop a phenomenological description of religiously significant conscious experience. The other more linguistic approach, sometimes referred to as Wittgensteinian fideism, proceeds by way of the analysis and description of the distinctive and irreducible character of religious discourse.

Four

PHENOMENOLOGY AND LINGUISTIC PHILOSOPHY OF RELIGION

Philosophical discussion about God, which today is more commonly referred to as philosophy of religion than as natural theology, has evolved from a pre-philosophical context and culture of religious belief. Religion, which precedes philosophy of religion, is conceived in a rather broad and nontechnical way as characterizing a specifically human activity. In general terms, it signifies the distinctive set of conscious relationships between human persons and a higher sacred reality or God. These include inner beliefs—sentiments, affections, desires, prayers, and so on—and outer professions—symbols, texts, rituals, worship, and so on. Also included is the regulation of personal and social lives inasmuch as they are valued as mediating or embodying valid relationships between persons and the sacred or, more specifically, between us and God.

Religion is at once cognitive and practical, a life of belief and a life of practical engagement that both nourish each other. It is profoundly self-involving—not just an abstract metaphysical account of a factual state of affairs. In professing my belief that I possess my being from God, I profess my personal radical dependence upon him. The God of religion is worshipped rather than just affirmed—a God of pre-philosophical culturally conditioned belief, conviction, and worship rather than a metaphysically derived conclusion.

In religion God is envisaged primarily in his relationship to humanity as its providential creator, sustainer, and final goal—not abstractly as he is in himself. Through "natural belief" or through "graced faith" (as in the main monotheist religions), God is affirmed as God-for-humanity. This God, the object of religious worship, is attained and affirmed primarily as corresponding and providing resolution to deep specifically human experiences such as those of finitude, insufficiency, contingency, fascination, dread, astonishment, hope, and desire. As John Smith elucidates, such worship characteristically involves a loving adhesion to an ideal form of life, an associated awareness of a chasm between this envisaged ideal and the imperfect quality of actual life, and recourse to a source of deliverance that overcomes the imperfection and accomplishes effective realization of the ideal.[1] For many—perhaps most—contemporary theistic philosophers, the philosophical elucidation of the God of religious belief, the God-for-us, is best achieved by way of phenomenological or linguistic description and analysis rather than by way of metaphysical argument.

Phenomenology of Religion

The philosophical method of phenomenology interprets all beings in terms of and from the viewpoint of their manifestation as phenomena appearing to individual human consciousness or subjectivity, not metaphysically in terms of their distinctively self-possessed being. Any being, which is thus affirmed as given

1. John Smith, *Experience and God* (Oxford: Oxford University Press, 1968), ch. 6.

correlatively to human consciousness, must, for phenomenology, always be considered and appraised solely from this standpoint. It is a philosophy of cognitional immanence in which any object of consciousness is affirmed not as it is independently in itself but as it is given to human consciousness. Thus for Husserl, its founding father, the reductive technique characteristic of contemporary phenomenology requires that any reference to transcendence must always be understood as transcendence within immanence.[2]

An object of religious consciousness is accessible phenomenologically only as an object of human consciousness, never as something enjoying intrinsic independent ontological significance. (Even if it is affirmed as existing independently, it is so affirmed only as thus appearing or given to human consciousness.) This emphasis of phenomenology on human consciousness or subjectivity should not be construed as embracing a merely subjectivist outlook. The phenomenological subject is affirmed as a being in the world—in virtue of whom and to whom a world, as this being's correlative other, deploys itself and becomes accessible. The subject is essentially a subject to whom a world becomes manifest, an intentional ex-static world-disclosing subject. The known world is other than the conscious subjectivity that knows it. However, this otherness of the world is such only as an otherness that is intrinsically correlative to the conscious subjectivity to which it is given. The intending subject and the world it discloses, *noesis* and *noema*, are distinct but intrinsically related. As Dan Zahavi remarks, "The relation between mind and the world is an internal one, a relation constitutive of its relata, and not an external one of causality."[3]

2. Edmund Husserl, *Ideas: General Introduction to Pure Phenomenology*, trans. W. Boyce Gibson (New York: Collier Books, 1962), 86.

3. Dan Zahavi, "Phenomenology," in *The Routledge Companion to Twentieth Century Philosophy*, ed. Dermot Moran (London: Routledge, 2008), 674.

Phenomenology is concerned with investigating and describing the ways and various modes in which different phenomena can manifest themselves to human consciousness (e.g., as perception, imagination, memory, desire). To accomplish this investigation, it suspends our "naïve" natural inclination to take for granted the intrinsically independent reality and intelligibility of the world. This suspension of the natural attitude is called the *epoche* or, more comprehensively, the phenomenological reduction. It is a bracketing or provisional suspension of the spontaneous assumptions and metaphysical presuppositions of the natural attitude, such as the autonomous existence, independent of our consciousness, of beings of various kinds and degrees of perfection. This method achieves a reduction or leading back, a *re-ductio* or return, to a presupposition-less world in which a strict correlativity of knowing and known obtains, and in which the being of things is methodologically identified with its manifestation to consciousness. The phenomenologist concentrates upon a first-person perspective that enables attention to be focused on an investigation of reality as it is given in its manifestation to, and its significance for, human consciousness—given as the intrinsic correlative of this attentive intending consciousness.

This phenomenological approach is well-adapted to undertake consideration of religion conceived as an essentially first-person self-involving relationship with God—a God "intended" and worshipped precisely as correlative and corresponding to the deepest conscious needs and desires of persons for meaning and value in their lives. It is an approach developed by many contemporary philosophers among whom Emmanuel Levinas, Paul Ricoeur, Richard Kearney, John Caputo, and Jean-Luc Marion are representative examples.

Typically, in such an approach, the reality of God is philosophically confirmed not by way of objective metaphysical argument as transcendent cause of the world but as shown to be implicated and operative in significant and often disconcerting human experiences. For example, Emmanuel Levinas argues that a philosophically persuasive affirmation of God can be attained only in the context of the ethical relationship between persons. This relationship, properly understood, is the primary irreducible structure that confers upon theological concepts the only significance they have. "Ethics is the spiritual optics.... There can be no 'knowledge' of God separated from the relationship with men. The Other is the very locus of metaphysical truth, and is indispensable for my relation with God."[4] For Levinas, the experience of an ethical relationship with another person, when accurately described phenomenologically, discloses a paradoxical asymmetry. Ethically the other person is experienced not just as an equivalent member of the same species or totality but as a unique Other to whom I find myself absolutely obligated. I find my center of gravity outside myself in the asymmetrical obligating requirement of the Other—widow, orphan, or beggar—an obligation recognized as unconditional demand and not just as the mirror image of the other's presumed obligation to me.

In this experience—which Levinas describes metaphorically as "the curvature of intersubjective space"—"being" or "reality" is apprehended as not simply an indifferent totality of equivalent parts. Undoubtedly the human race is a biological species, and in respect to common functions that people may exercise in the world as members of the same species, people can be considered under a common concept. But the essence of society is not like a species

4. Emmanuel Levinas, *Totality and Infinity*, trans. Alphonso Lingis (Pittsburgh: Duquesne University Press, 1969), 78.

that unites interchangeable similar individuals. It is not comparable to the collectivity of a beehive. It is "the intersubjective experience that leads to the social experience and endows it with meaning (as to believe the phenomenologist, perception, impossible to conjure away, endows scientific experience with meaning)."[5]

The Other resists and calls into question my power, not by opposing a greater force than mine within the totality of forces but by the infinity of his transcendence, which prior to any struggle or war finds expression in his face as the primordial word: "you shall not commit murder."[6] This experience of the Other as a surplus beyond the *a priori* resources of thought is an absolutely innovative experience. It discloses a radical multiplicity irreducible to numerical multiplicity, an asymmetrical pluralism irreducible to any totality of mutually defining parts.

The Other, encountered primordially as transcendent yet destitute, does not limit my freedom but promotes it, nonviolently, by arousing my goodness. "Goodness," Levinas remarks, "consists in taking up a position in being such that the Other counts more than myself."[7] Morality arises not as a calculus of equality but from the fact that infinite exigencies concerning the service of others converge at one point of the universe—myself.[8] For Levinas, a religious relationship with God is achieved through such ethical relationships with other people. The ethical relationship in which the individual subject acknowledges concretely the irreducible moral claims of the Other is in its deepest significance the relationship between a person and the transcendent God, and as thus envisaged is what we call religion. Levinas speaks of the dimension of the di-

5. Ibid., 53.
6. Ibid., 199.
7. Ibid., 245.
8. Ibid.

vine being manifest in the human face of the stranger, the widow, and the orphan who solicit us in their destitution. God is supremely present as the ultimate significance of the justice that we render to other persons. Our relationship with him is more effectively disclosed in our ethical welcome of the Other than by any attempt to comprehend his transcendence theoretically. To expand upon the passage already quoted:

Ethics is the spiritual optics.... There can be no "knowledge" of God separated from the relationship with men.... The dimension of the divine opens forth from the human face.... God rises to his supreme and ultimate presence as correlative to the justice rendered unto men.... The Other is not the incarnation of God, but precisely by his face, in which he is disincarnate, is the very manifestation of the height in which God is revealed.[9]

The basic contention of Levinas is that an effective affirmation of God is accessible only by way of phenomenological description and analysis of the ethical relationship with the Other. It is not to be attained by way of traditional metaphysical reasoning, which he calls "ontology" and which differs significantly from the genuine metaphysics achieved in the phenomenological account of the ethical relationship. The ontology typical of traditional metaphysics has characteristically aspired to a speculative comprehension of being as such. It subordinates otherness and exteriority to sameness within a unifying horizon or concept of being. "*Being* before the *existent*, ontology before metaphysics, is freedom (be it the freedom of theory) before justice. It is a movement within the same before obligation to the other."[10] This "freedom of theory" is not a positive one because it is the face of the Other that is meant to bind

9. Ibid., 78–80.
10. Ibid., 47.

the self to both ethical action and a metaphysics based on ethics. Instead of theory, for Levinas, the divine reality is disclosed in genuine metaphysics (i.e., phenomenology) as the profound meaning of the asymmetrical curvature of intersubjective space that characterizes the ethical relationship in which the Other is placed "higher" than me—in the sense that my ethical responsibility for him is more than I can require of him for myself. "This 'curvature' of space," Levinas says, "is perhaps, the very presence of God."[11]

This claim that a cognitive religious relationship with God is disclosed in our ethical relationships with other people may strike a responsive chord in anyone already committed to the Judeo-Christian teaching that access to God cannot be disassociated from loving welcome of one's neighbor. But further consideration will be required to persuade others, who may be sympathetic to Levinas's conception of the ethical relationship, that it does in fact imply the religious significance that he ascribes to it.

In the course of several works, Richard Kearney has developed a similar approach to a philosophical affirmation of God, an approach both required and appropriate in what he recognizes is a largely post-theistic culture. He discards the traditional arguments "proving" the existence of an all-powerful creator. It is "farewell to the old God of metaphysical power, the God we thought we knew and possessed, the omni-God of sovereignty and theodicy. Adieu, therefore, to the God that Nietzsche, Freud, and Marx declared dead."[12]

He argues that the only God recoverable today is a God for man—a God essentially and correlatively linked to human aspira-

11. Ibid., 291.

12. Richard Kearney, *Reimagining the Sacred*, ed. Kearney and Jens Zimmermann (New York: Columbia University Press, 2016), 17.

tions. "God does not reveal himself, therefore, as an essence *in se* but as an I-Self for us. . . . The God of Mosaic manifestation cannot be God without relating to his other—humanity."[13] This God for man is welcomed as a possibility—a call, a cry, or summons—that enables us to accomplish, beyond our limited self-regarding propensities, an ethical order of justice and love. The paradigm of this rediscovery of the sacred is our hazardous loving welcome of the stranger, the alien, and the impoverished. Such welcome by us is facilitated and enabled by a sensitive phenomenological interpretation of various texts that disclose to us evidence of divine transcendence, immanent within experience, enabling a profoundly ethical response in challenging and mysterious circumstances (e.g., Abraham's hospitable welcome of the three strangers, Mary's trusting acceptance of the angel Gabriel's invitation).

Genuine faith is portrayed by Kearney not as a propositional belief *that* God exists but as faith *in* an infinite demand, desire, hope, trust. This involves a more phenomenological, hermeneutical, and practically relevant affirmation of God. It is a challenge to locate the sacred within the secular, to welcome divine transcendence within human immanence. By welcoming the sacred as an ethically enabling possibility beyond our ordinary capacity, we accomplish the kingdom of God. We actualize the God who may be, who invokes us as an eschatological, or yet to be actualized, possibility. We make actual the divine possibility that God is for us.

This orientation of talk about God to concrete human experience yields many rich and revealing insights about the practical implications of religion as a way of life rather than as an abstract metaphysical speculation. Although at first sight strange, many

13. Richard Kearney, *The God Who May Be* (Bloomington: Indiana University Press, 2001), 21–22.

of the claims about us enabling God to be—"God is up to us in the end"—can be given a perfectly intelligible meaning.[14] Undoubtedly we humans must exist if God is to be a God for us. And it is as thus correlative to us that Kearney's hermeneutical phenomenology can advance illuminating considerations about rediscovering God in our anatheistic (or post-theistic) times. Phenomenological and hermeneutical interpretation of historico-religious texts can provide an illuminating account of how God can become a reality for us as an ethical inspiration in our lives. However, the question remains whether God's correlativity to us is absolute, but we must return to this question later for it involves meta-phenomenological or metaphysical issues.

A similar phenomenological approach to religious claims is suggested by Paul Ricoeur. He addresses the issue of how a conscious subject might properly claim to experience some awareness of a divine reality without simply inventing it. If what is represented in experience, the *noema,* is correlative to the intentionality, *noesis,* of the knowing subject—which, ever since Kant, claims some mastery over the meaning of its experience—how can we claim to know that the significance of an alleged experience of the divine is not merely a representation constituted and determined by the conscious subject of the experience?

Ricoeur replies that there are feelings and dispositions that can be called "religious" that "can transgress the sway of representation and, in this sense, mark the subject's being overthrown from its ascendancy in the realm of meaning."[15] What is given as profoundly meaningful experience is apprehended as not of our own making or

14. Kearney, *Reimagining the Sacred,* 250.

15. Paul Ricoeur, "Experience and Language in Religious Discourse," in *Phenomenology and the Theological Turn: The French Debate*, ed. Janicaud Dominique, trans. Bernard G. Prusak and Jeffrey L. Kosky (New York: Fordham University Press, 2000), 127.

invention. For example, there is the feeling of absolute dependence (Schleiermacher); the feeling of utter confidence, in spite of everything (Barth and Bultmann); the feeling of ultimate concern (Paul Tillich); the feeling of being preceded in the order of speech, love, and existence (Rosenzweig).

These feelings, which are ways of being absolutely affected, bear witness to the inability of our intentionality to constitute a consciousness of something wholly other. The fundamental disposition that corresponds to these feelings and affections can be seen as "prayer" in its various forms, such as complaint, supplication, demand, and praise. This religious response of prayerful obedience to a call must be distinguished from the problem-solving response to a question or problematic situation. We must clearly distinguish the epistemological relation between question and reply from the religious relation between call and obedient response where the superiority of the call is recognized and avowed.

Prayer turns to this Other by whom conscious feeling is affected, and this Other that affects it is apperceived as the source of the call to which prayer responds. Hence Ricoeur concludes: "I therefore grant unreservedly that there can be a phenomenology of feelings and dispositions that can be qualified as religious by virtue of the disproportion within the relation between call and response. This phenomenology would not be merely descriptive but critical, as I just suggested."[16]

This theme of providing a philosophical validation of a religious affirmation of God by way of a phenomenological account of awareness of a divine reality is developed most influentially and effectively by Jean Luc Marion. He likewise challenges the tradition deriving from Descartes through Kant and Husserl that sees

16. Ibid., 128.

the intending subject as constituting or establishing rigorous preconditions for the manifestation and appearance of phenomena that are intuited. He concedes that what is intuited often falls short of what is intentionally envisaged. We impose further significance upon what is given perceptually; for example, we envisage as traffic lights our perception of three colored lights. Similarly, we sometimes envisage what has no possibility of intuitive fulfillment—for example, we might try to envisage a square circle.

However, we can envisage a third possibility described by Marion as follows: "The intention (the concept or the signification) can never reach adequation with the intuition (fulfillment), not because the latter is lacking but because it exceeds what the concept can receive, expose, and comprehend."[17] He calls this excess of intuition over intention the "saturated phenomenon." The giving intuition exceeds, submerges, and saturates the measure of any concept. What we experience is more than we can express conceptually.

For Marion, every phenomenon or manifestation that shows itself does so to the extent that it gives itself first. This implies that the subject of experience is no longer seen as wholly or primarily determining the conditions of the possibility of experience, that is, of phenomenality. What is given in experience does indeed require as its counterpart the "given to" pole of subjectivity, the *noesis* of the *noema*, to phenomenalize the given. But this subjectivity does not precede the phenomenon as though constituting the preconditions of its appearance. In thus according an active, indeed primary, role to what is given in experience, the way is opened for Marion's characteristic claim that what is intuited can exceed, overflow,

<hr/>

17. Jean-Luc Marion, *God, the Gift, and Postmodernism*, ed. John D. Caputo and Michael J. Scanlon (Bloomington: Indiana University Press, 1999), 39.

and utterly saturate the subject's capacity to envisage, intend, or conceptualize it.

This initiates the possibility of a new dimension of phenomenology, one that is open to a phenomenological intuition of the divine. We discover that "access to the divine phenomenality is not forbidden to man."[18] There remains, whether by way of revelation or natural affection, the possibility of an intuitively experienced divine gift or givenness of such bedazzling, superabundant, unconditional perfection and saturating impact that no intention or concept or signification can organize, contain, or foresee it. "In short God remains incomprehensible, not imperceptible—without adequate concept, not without giving intuition."[19]

Marion's subtle account of saturated phenomena is intended to delineate the possibility of a phenomenologically given intuition of God such as one finds (but not exclusively) in descriptions of mystical experience. Although this account affirms an intuition of God, it also claims to defend an affirmation of divine transcendence. It argues that the subject is rendered wholly receptive vis-à-vis any such saturating self-revelation of the divine. It is "reduced" to the status of a secondary or derived subject, constituted rather than constituting. It becomes a *me* rather than an *I*, bereft of any limiting claim to be the ultimate foundation of the experience of phenomena. *I* do not lay hold of the transcendent. It lays hold of *me*.

But how, one might ask, can what is experienced or perceived be wholly transcendent if it is somehow calibrated with or correlative to a perceiving human subject? Would it not be more plausible to identify the allegedly dazzling experience as a pre-reflective consciousness of the intensity of our own act of awareness rather than

18. Ibid., 41.
19. Ibid., 40.

74

as a direct perception of divine transcendence? Perhaps what is sometimes pre-reflectively apperceived or affirmed as "saturated" or "dazzling" is our own act of perceiving rather than a directly perceived dazzling divine object or God. On some occasions, our own assent and adhesion to what we claim to believe or affirm may be joyfully apprehended as a "dazzling" or "saturating" or profoundly assuring conviction. What dazzles or saturates is not a given divine reality but the intensity and conviction of my assent to the authenticity or truth of what is affirmed or envisaged. The object thus affirmed or envisaged, however assuredly, may remain obscure, mysterious, and incomprehensible. The given that is experienced is a convincing created cipher or trace of God's transcendence, a reliable basis perhaps for an act of faith or a causal metaphysical argument, rather than a directly perceived saturating and dazzlingly evident experience of God's divine transcendence itself.

Linguistic Philosophy of Religion

Before offering some reflections on the phenomenological approach to the philosophy of religion espoused by the philosophers considered above, I wish to outline briefly a comparable and closely related approach that was influential in the late twentieth-century British linguistic philosophy of religion. This approach, like the phenomenological approach, discounts the relevance of metaphysical argument. It confines philosophical discussion of the affirmation of God to its role within the religious form of life and language where alone, it is alleged, such discussion makes sense. This religious form of life and language establishes its own internal criteria of rationality, one which is logically unamenable to any external assessment or confirmation. Its guiding inspiration is the Wittgensteinian suggestion that many seemingly deep problems are not metaphysical issues about what really exists or how things are but conceptual problems about appropriate linguistic usage. In the case of theistic beliefs or assertions, it is argued that such beliefs are intrinsically but nonproblematically groundless. They are to be understood as primarily grammatical assertions rather than as ontological ones—ways in which believers find they must speak about their religious belief rather than objective metaphysical statements about the structure of reality.

Norman Malcolm provides a forthright defense of the nonproblematic groundlessness of theistic belief. It is nonproblematic because most of our important beliefs are likewise groundless and incapable of independent confirmation or proof. Consider, for example, our belief that familiar things such as watches, shoes, and wallets do not cease to exist without some physical explanation. We are convinced that they do not just pop out of existence even though we have had the experience of things being lost and not turning up again. A society that believed that things could simply "vanish into thin air" would differ from us greatly in their attachment to things, in their persistence in searching, and in their appraisal of evidence of theft. Yet we never try to support with reason our fundamental conviction that things don't simply cease to exist without trace. It is tacitly accepted as an unquestioned element of the fundamental framework of our thinking about material things. "We are taught, or we absorb, the system within which we raise doubts, make enquiries, draw conclusions. We grow into a framework. We don't question it. We accept it trustingly."[20]

In view of the pervasive acceptance of groundless belief, it is

---

20. Norman Malcolm, "The Groundlessness of Belief," in *Reason and Religion*, ed. Stuart C. Brown (Ithaca, N.Y.: Cornell University Press, 1977), 147.

maintained that there should be nothing surprising or disconcerting about the claim that religious belief is also an instance of
groundless belief. Religious belief is a perspective on reality, which
is not like a hypothesis for or against which evidence can be mar-
shaled. We cannot prove its truth to others: we can only invite them
to share the vision and nurture it by illuminating examples. Mal-
com continues, "In brief 'religion' is a form of life, it is a language
embedded in action—what Wittgenstein called a 'language game.'
Science is another. Neither stands in need of justification, the one
no more than the other."[21]

In another essay in the same book, Colin Lyas refines this
approach by distinguishing between regulative and constitutive
framework principles of a belief system. Regulative principles are
widely accepted principles within a belief system that may in fact
change from time to time by way of radical innovation within the
system—as, for example, the change within science from a Ptole-
maic to a Copernican conception of the universe. The constitutive
principles define the system and "are groundless in that our only
reply when asked to justify them is that without them justification
makes no sense. They are what 'Justification' means."[22] For example, a groundless constitutive principle of the belief system of science is the affirmation that "if there is a contradiction in a scientific theory, it is worthless."

Lyas goes on to affirm that a religious belief system similarly
involves groundless framework constitutive principles. "It not
merely *does not* but *could not* rise or fall on the basis of grounds or
evidence."[23] For, he explains, a genuinely theistic belief is distinc-

---

21. Malcolm, "The Groundlessness of Belief," 156.

22. Colin Lyas, "The Groundlessness of Religious Belief," in *Reason and Religion*,
ed. Stuart C. Brown (Ithaca, N.Y.: Cornell University Press, 1977), 169.

23. Ibid., 179–80.

tively and characteristically such that it enables one to respond to the vicissitudes and contingencies of the world with an assurance that one has recourse to a source of security, which comes to one not from anything in oneself or the world and which guarantees one's safety whatever may happen in the world. This could not be the case if this theistic belief were vulnerable to the outcome of fallible attempts to establish by indirect metaphysical argument the probable existence of a religiously adequate God. It is inconsistent to maintain both that one holds a genuinely theistic belief and that it is appropriate to seek independent evidence to rationally justify it.

A similar approach to the groundlessness of theistic belief based on grammatical considerations is advocated by D. Z. Philips. God's existence, he claims, is not something that anyone could find out by way of arriving at a matter-of-fact answer. It makes no sense to envisage God's existence as either a fact or not a fact to which some process of rational argument might be relevant in deciding which alternative might be true. The question of the reality of God is a question of the possibility of sense and nonsense, truth and falsity, *in religion.*

In coming to see through religion that there is a God, one does not come to see that an additional being exists whose existence might be independently established. One comes rather to see a new meaning in one's life and to attain a new kind of understanding. Discovering that there is a God is not like establishing that something exists within a familiar universe of discourse. Rather, it is a discovery of a new universe of discourse. We must not suppose that God's reality is to be construed as an existent among existents. As Kierkegaard put it: "God does not exist: He is eternal."[24] See-

24. Soren Kierkegaard, *Concluding Unscientific Postscript*, trans. David Swenson and Walter Lowrie (Princeton: Princeton University Press, 1941), 296.

ing that there is a God is synonymous with seeing the possibility of eternal love. If one rises above the dimensions of contingent temporal love, such as self-love, erotic love, and friendship, to an acknowledgment that there is an eternal love that will not let one go whatever happens, one thereby attains the affirmation of God. In the context of religion—which is the only one appropriate to a discussion of God—belief, understanding, and love can be equated.

For Philips the arguments of natural theology are both irrelevant and potentially misleading. The truths of religious discourse arise only within commitment to a religious form of life, and it is misleading to look for philosophical arguments that would establish their truth or even their possible truth. It is a basic mistake to suppose that "the relation between religious beliefs and the non-religious facts is that between what is justified and its justification, or that between a conclusion and its grounds."[25]

For such linguistic philosophers of religion, there are no trans-field criteria of rationality through which the truths of theistic discourse, which arise only in religion, could be evaluated. These truths can be fully understood and assessed only through an insider's grasp of the religious form of life of which they are a part. "Religious language is not an interpretation of how things are but determines how things are for the believer."[26] There can be no philosophical justification of commitment to God outside the religious form of life of which this commitment is a part.

Further refinement of this approach is provided by Peter Winch.[27] He seeks to undermine the view that a religious belief is

25. D. Z. Philips, *Faith and Philosophical Enquiry* (London: Routledge and Kegan Paul, 1970), 101.

26. Ibid., 101.

27. Peter Winch, "Meaning and Religious Language," in *Reason and Religion*, ed. Stuart C. Brown, 193–221 (Ithaca, N.Y.: Cornell University Press, 1977).

lacking in meaning and rationality unless it involves theological presuppositions that commit the believer to verifiable or at least falsifiable existential claims. Religious worship and practice, involving certain characteristic uses of language, is a basic primitive human response to certain distinctive human situations and predicaments such as a profound sense of dependence or an encounter with affliction. The application of theological doctrines must be understood within the context, and within the grammatical constraints, of the characteristic language of such worship and practice. It would be a mistake to regard them as independently articulating a *theory* about the nature of the world.

Ceasing to believe in the existence of God cannot be separated from ceasing to see the point of prayer and worship, for they constitute the context within which the affirmation finds application. Seeing or ceasing to see any point in prayer and worship is a *constitutive aspect* of believing or ceasing to believe in God. The world of experience with all its vicissitudes provides the factual circumstances in which the affirmation of the existence of God finds application. This does not mean that this affirmation refers simply to these circumstances but rather that the reality that it expresses is disclosed by the way it understands and interprets these circumstances. He quotes with approval Simone Weil's remark: "Earthly things are the criterion of spiritual things. . . . Only spiritual things are of value, but only physical things have a verifiable existence. Therefore the value of the former can only be verified as an illumination projected onto the latter."[28] The upshot of Winch's argument is that a properly philosophical appraisal of religious discourse would reveal that its "relation to reality" is to be understood

---

28. Simone Weil, *First and Last Notebooks*, trans. Rush Rees (London: Oxford University Press, 1970), 147.

in terms of its application within lived experience rather than in terms of its reference to a "different order of reality" beyond such experience. And it is in this manner that a believer's natural and unconfused recourse to expressions such as "a higher reality" or "not of this world" should be understood. "Religious uses of language, I want to say, are not descriptions of an 'order of reality' distinct from the earthly life with which we are familiar. . . . These uses of language do, however, have an application in what religious people say and do in the course of their life on earth and this is where their 'relation to reality' is to be sought."[29]

There are significant similarities between the phenomenological and linguistic approaches to the philosophy of religion outlined above, despite their differences in emphasis on the individual's experience or the community's language and practice. They both dismiss the relevance of metaphysics or traditional "natural theology," and they both argue for an exclusively anthropocentric or human-subject-related conception of theism. I propose to consider first their shared anthropocentric conception of theism. This will prepare the way for a subsequent appraisal of their dismissal of the role of metaphysics or natural theology in the philosophy of religion.

29. Winch, "Meaning and Religious Language," 214.

Five

ANTHROPOCENTRIC THEISM

For and Against

The anthropocentric conception of theism maintains that any philosophical affirmation of God must be understood in the context and terms of the resources and circumstance of human consciousness. God is affirmed not as an independently existing reality but as corresponding and providing resolution to specifically human profound experiences such as those of finitude, concern, awe, dependence, vulnerability, exaltation, or saturating givenness. Thus Richard Kearney remarks that "the God of Mosaic manifestation cannot be god without relating to his other—humanity."[1] And for Marion, divine transcendence is given in experience as a structure immanent to human consciousness. "I make it my goal to establish that givenness remains an immanent structure of any kind of phenomenality, whether immanent or transcendent."[2] Likewise, for linguistic philosophers such as Philips, the truths of religious discourse such as the affirmation of God must be understood and assessed exclusively within a grasp of the religious form of life that they are a part of. "Religious language is not an interpretation of

---

1. Kearney, *The God Who May Be*, 22.
2. Marion, *God, The Gift, and Postmodernism*, 70.

how things are. It determines how things are for the believer."[3]

It seems to me that what is involved in both such approaches is an acceptance of the primacy of the correlationist principle, which, as I indicated earlier, has been described as a defining feature of philosophy since the epistemological arguments of Kant in the nineteenth century. Recall Quentin Meillassoux's claim that "the central notion of modern philosophy since Kant seems to be that of *correlation*. By 'correlation' we mean the idea according to which we only ever have access to the correlation between thinking and being, and never to either term considered apart from the other. . . . Every philosophy which disavows naïve realism has become a variant of correlationism."[4]

The way in which both phenomenology and the Wittgensteinian linguistic philosophy of religion maintain that any affirmation of the existence of God is intrinsically relative to human consciousness and experience clearly qualifies them as examples of such correlationism. From such a perspective, it is difficult to discern in what sense the divine reality might be affirmed as somehow independent of this correlation with humanity, as is certainly affirmed within various creedal formulations of religious belief. It would be difficult, for example, to reply to Merleau-Ponty's remark that one can never be sure whether it is God who sustains men in their human reality or vice versa, since his existence is affirmed only via their own.[5]

However, this only becomes a significant philosophical problem if, as sometimes seems to be the case, this alleged divine correlativity is accorded exclusive and unqualified significance. It

3. Philips, *Faith and Philosophical Enquiry*, 101.
4. Quentin Meillassoux, *After Finitude*, 5.
5. Maurice Merleau-Ponty, *Eloge de la philosophie* (Paris: Gallimard, 1958), 38.

is of course true, indeed a truism, that "there can be no religious discourse about or belief in God as existing independently—apart from a believing subject." But this is not equivalent to maintaining that there can be no religious discourse about or belief in God—as existing independently apart from a believing subject. The latter statement is not a truism. It is false. The point can be made more generally and obviously by the consideration that the truism "Nothing can be known or intuited as independently existing—apart from a knowing subject" does not imply that "Nothing can be known or intuited—as independently existing apart from a knowing subject."

We must distinguish between a realist metaphysical account of what is given fundamentally to a conscious subject and a phenomenological account of the same. For the realist metaphysician, what is given is intuited as existing independently of its givenness to consciousness. For the phenomenologist, what is given is perceived only as being given to consciousness. For the metaphysician, what is involved is an asymmetrical relationship. For the phenomenologist, the relationship is one of strict correlation—even if, as Marion appears to maintain, the noematic given term of the relation is affirmed as active and the noetic given-to conscious subject is affirmed only as passive.

The distinction comes down to the difference between phenomenology on the one hand—which, in virtue of its bracketing from consideration the intrinsic independent existence of what we perceive experientially, is thereby committed to correlationism—and a realist philosophy on the other—which, in affirming as intuitively evident this self-possessed independent existence, is not so committed. Can a God, accessible philosophically only and exclusively as a phenomenon situated within human experience or discourse, however passively experienced as a saturating givenness, be affirmed to really exist independently or be utterly transcendent? To maintain that God exists independently and is integrally transcendent would seem to imply that he is unbounded by any human experience—yet it is precisely and only as appearing within or as given to human experience that he is affirmed by phenomenology and some strands of linguistic philosophy. The claim that he is experienced therein as radically transcendent must face the difficulty that this transcendence, however sublime, is affirmed as a reality only as given immanently to human consciousness, however passively envisaged.

Although it is true that religious belief affirms God as corresponding efficaciously to human concerns, this need not imply that God can only be affirmed as so corresponding. Indeed, the God religiously envisaged as corresponding to human exigencies can also be philosophically and theologically envisaged as enjoying independent, unlimited transcendent existence. The correlationist language appropriate to religious belief may not be appropriate or adequate to this latter consideration for which a more impersonal metaphysical discourse may be required.

In most areas of discourse, including that concerning the affirmation of God, there are at least two appropriate ways in which a topic can be considered. For example, my account of my perception of a beautiful sunset will differ from a neurologist's account of the experience. On the one hand is the internal or subject-related account, and on the other is the external and impersonally objective consideration. The two accounts are autonomous, incomplete, but complementary. They see the world differently, but they are not different worlds. They are irreducible to one another, each attaining significant insights but at the expense of abstracting from those of the other. My account of my aesthetic experience of the beautiful sunset is not reducible without residue to the neurologist's account of it, and her account is not a reproduction of my personal aesthetic experience, which she deciphers or interprets impersonally. The accounts' selective characters, which enable their differing stances and discourses, also constitute the basis for a discussion of their compatibility and complementarity.

From the external or objective viewpoint, we seek, as far as possible, to describe and understand a world as it exists independently of our pre-scientific and pre-philosophical personal perspective on it. We seek to adopt what Thomas Nagel has called "the view from nowhere." It is the viewpoint characteristic of natural science, notably physics (which itself resorts to complementary terminologies of waves and particles to account for mundane phenomena such as radiation and light). This characteristic external or objective viewpoint of natural science is also characteristic of realist metaphysics, which not only affirms the independent extra-mental existence of the world but also proposes and evaluates the objective reflective arguments that claim to confirm the existence of God as the world's ultimate creator and explanation. Such objective metaphysical inquiry seeks to determine the ontological structure of finite being, to establish its created dependence upon God (appropriately identified as infinite being), and to develop an objective account of the coexistence of finite being and infinite being. This inquiry insists that a comprehensive discussion of creation cannot bracket out or ignore these metaphysical assertions about the ontological status of creatures, of God, and of their relationship.

In sharp contrast to this "external" and objective metaphysical approach, we have seen how the phenomenological (and also the "linguistic") approach to God adopts a distinctly more "internal" and subject-oriented perspective. The difference between the two

approaches, the metaphysical and the phenomenological, is highlighted by their differing accounts of divine transcendence.

In realist metaphysics, this transcendence is understood impersonally and objectively as involving a radical asymmetry between God and the world that we experience. This asymmetry
emphasizes God's radical ontological independence of this world,
which is understood as related to him as his freely enacted and
totally dependent creation. Metaphysically, God's immanence is
affirmed only in terms of his sustaining activity, which maintains
this freely created world in existence as totally dependent upon and
relative to his absolute transcendence of it. Metaphysically understood, the divine nature exists independently of creation. We know
that God exists by argument from his creation. But *pace* Hegel, who
claimed that "without the world God would not be God"—had there
been no creation, God would still be God.

By contrast, in Marion's phenomenology, this metaphysical
understanding of divine transcendence and immanence appears
to be reversed. Divine transcendence is identified as a saturated
phenomenon experienced as given *within* the context of its alleged
immanence to human awareness ("I make it my goal to establish
that givenness remains an immanent structure of any kind of
phenomenality, whether immanent or transcendent"). It appears
to be an epistemological rather than a metaphysical conception
of divine transcendence. In this conception, God's independent
transcendence of the intrinsic resources and constitutive activity
of our conscious subjectivity is certainly still affirmed. However,
his independent transcendence is affirmed only as related to this
conscious subjectivity, which is thereby enabled to phenomenalize
it passively as a given and saturating intuitive experience of divine
transcendence. "The constituting subject is succeeded by the con-

stituted witness. As constituted witness the subject remains the worker of truth, but is no longer its producer."[6]

What is involved here in such phenomenological affirmation of divine transcendence is a replacement of the metaphysical principle of efficient or creative causation by an epistemological principle of sufficient intuition. The phenomenologist believes that by denying any active or constitutive role to the passive subject of the intuitively given saturating awareness of divine transcendence, she is justified in affirming that she enjoys a genuine uncontrived phenomenological experience of God's independently possessed transcendence. The metaphysician can reply, correctly in my view, that there can be no direct phenomenological experience of God's independently possessed transcendence, however dazzling or obscure, and that whatever seems to be so experienced is, at best, a trace or cipher or created effect of this transcendence, whose real existence must be established by indirect metaphysical causal argument. It is not sufficient to affirm that phenomenologically God's transcendence is experienced, intuited, or perceived immanently *as if* or *as though* absolutely independent. This "as if" or "as though" must be transformed philosophically into an affirmation of objective reality by independent causal metaphysical argument.

Speaking uncritically, one might perhaps say that divine transcendence is *exemplified* in such experienced ciphers, traces, or effects. But it is certainly not *instantiated* therein, as some phenomenological accounts appear to suggest. The finite exemplifications of divine transcendence disclosed, for example, in mystical experience or in our more commonplace experiences of radical dependence, contingency, and longing, must be metaphysically

6. Jean-Luc Marion, *The Visible and the Revealed*, trans. Christina Gschwandtner et al. (New York: Fordham University Press, 2008), 44.

deciphered. This is achieved by a causal metaphysical argument that concludes that there exists, as the creative cause of what is thus experienced, a nonexperienced infinite instantiation of independently possessed divine transcendence. In the absence of such a metaphysical argument, one would have to rely upon the gift of faith alone, to the exclusion of any philosophical consideration of natural reason, to acknowledge God's objective and independently possessed divine transcendence.

The difficulty with the phenomenological viewpoint (and also with the linguistic viewpoint that claims that the truths of religious discourse arise exclusively within a religious form of life) is that it tends to represent God exclusively as a *correlative* given to human consciousness, however passive and unproductive this conscious subject may be described. The challenge is, as Meillassoux puts it "to break with the ontological requisite of the moderns, according to which to be is *to be a correlate*."[7]

We must seek to understand and explain how thought is able to access God as uncorrelated: in other words, how God can exist, and be affirmed to exist, without being given to human consciousness. We must show how God exists as absolute and not only as given correlatively to human consciousness, however significant such givenness is for religious belief. We must show how God exists as nonrelative to us, and so exists whether or not we exist. Religious belief and discourse about God, which envisage him as corresponding and correlative to our deepest exigencies, however religiously illuminating and inspiring, must be qualified and complemented by an account of our radical dependence upon his absolute nonrelative and independently possessed existence. It is through indirect metaphysical argument that such an account may be developed.

7. Meillassoux, *After Finitude*, 28.

The difficulty that the phenomenological approach appears to encounter with the metaphysical is grounded in its own unconditional "turning away from" or "putting between brackets of" the natural standpoint. This affects the reduction to immanence of all transcendent objects that present themselves as real from the natural "standpoint." At the heart of this replacement of the moderate realist natural standpoint is a replacement of the metaphysical concept of "substance" by that of "conscious subject," which exists only as a term in an internal conscious relationship with a "given" that situates it.

For metaphysics, substance is the radical intrinsic principle or cause of being in the things that exist. It is the origin of the resources that characterize a being—its nature, its qualities, and its activity. In the case of a human "being," its substance as individual self possesses the required resources and causal efficacy for the emergence and exercise of its characteristic activities of understanding and love. Consciousness is not what profoundly constitutes the being of the substantial self: rather, it is an activity distinct from and emerging from this substantial self.

My reality as existing substance precedes my phenomenological reality as intentional subjectivity and is not wholly reducible to phenomenology's discourse. Such discourse implies an order prior to itself, an ontological order of independently existing substances that is beyond the limited signifying capacity of phenomenological subjectivity to adequately express. Being and its phenomenological manifestation are always formally distinct. The ability of realist metaphysical discourse to signify the existent precisely as existing independently enables such discourse to engage with a world that transcends it. As Aquinas remarked pertinently from his pre-phenomenological perspective, "Concepts stand in relation to the intellect as that by which it thinks or understands and not as that of which it thinks."[8]

If, as I claim, such metaphysical consideration of being is of crucial importance in a philosophical defense of theism, and a necessary complement to any phenomenological presentation of religious belief and experience, it is important to indicate the nature and credibility of such metaphysical consideration. Because metaphysics is so out of favor in phenomenological circles as well as in others, this retrieval of metaphysics is not a very popular undertaking these days. Thus Richard Kearney bids "farewell to the old God of metaphysical power, the God we thought we knew and possessed, the omni-God of sovereignty and theodicy."[9] And for John Caputo: "With the withering away of Metaphysics ... we are free to return to the nourishment of the old religious narratives."[10]

However, encouraged by Etienne Gilson's remark that "metaphysics always buries its undertakers," I proceed now to a brief account of the relevance and justification of a metaphysical approach to key issues in philosophical theism.[11]

8. Aquinas, *Summa theologiae* I, q. 85, art. 2.

9. Kearney, *Reimagining the Sacred*, 17.

10. John Caputo and Gianni Vattimo, *After the Death of God* (New York: Columbia University Press, 2007), 75.

11. Etienne Gilson, *The Unity of Philosophical Experience* (San Francisco: Ignatius Press, 1999), 246. The direct quote is "Philosophy always buries its undertakers," but by philosophy, he means philosophy insofar as it includes metaphysics.

Six

THEISM AND METAPHYSICS

Metaphysical discussion of fundamental issues concerning the existence and nature of God and our coexistence with him is conducted in abstract, universal, and objective terms. Such metaphysical discourse differs sharply from the concrete, subject-oriented, and self-involving discourse of religious experience and belief, which is so perceptively elaborated by phenomenological description. The promotion of religious commitment is not the direct aim or object of metaphysical discussion about the existence and nature of God.

However, although metaphysics seeks to pursue an objective "view from nowhere" approach, it is not entirely detached from self-involving implications and consequences. To claim that "God created the world and everything therein" cannot be quite as disinterested an observation as to affirm that "Heat causes water to boil at 100 degrees centigrade at sea level." The former claim logically involves consequences for attitude and action for whoever affirms it in a way that the latter affirmation does not. For it logically involves that the person who affirms it acknowledges that she is radically dependent upon God for her existence and activity. The logical threads that lead her to an affirmation that a kettle in California will boil at a particular temperature are not similarly self-involving.

Indeed, it is precisely because a metaphysical affirmation of God has self-involving consequences for attitude and action that many unbelievers reject the affirmation. They maintain that such an affirmation undermines their freedom and autonomy. Thus, in the existentialism of Jean-Paul Sartre, even if a person were to judge himself to be created, as a *free* creature he would resolutely stand against God in radical independence. And for Merleau-Ponty: "The metaphysical and moral consciousness perishes at the touch of the Absolute."[1]

However, although the conclusion that God exists may raise the self-involving issue of how this conclusion affects the affirmation of human autonomy, the metaphysical argument for his existence is itself articulated in abstract and objective terms. In its different forms, the basic argument is that various aspects of the finite beings or substances of our experience are unintelligible and even contradictory unless they are understood to be created by God, who is envisaged as infinite being and is affirmed as existing independently of the universe of finite beings.

We experience this domain of finite beings as comprising different kinds of substances, substances that manifest differing characteristic tendencies and interactions. Various features of this universe of finite beings have served as points of departure for distinctive arguments for the existence of God, such as the Five Ways of proving the existence of God proposed by Thomas Aquinas. These include the aspects of change, dependency, contingency, hierarchical diversity, and goal-achieving activity that characterize the finite beings or substances that compose the universe of our experience. Each of these aspects can serve as the basis of an argu-

1. Maurice Merleau-Ponty, "Le Métaphysique dans l'homme," in *Sens et non-sens*, 3rd ed. (Paris: Gallimard, 1961), 167.

ment that concludes that the universe of finite beings is ultimately unintelligible and even contradictory unless it is acknowledged to be the radically dependent creation of infinite being.

The law-like orderly regularity of nature itself is for some the preferred basis of argument. It seeks to argue to the existence of God as the ultimate, necessary, and sufficient precondition of the possibility of such order. As John Haldane remarks, "They reason that, while events in nature can be explained by reference to the fundamental particles and the laws under which they operate, natural science cannot explain these factors. Natural explanations having reached their logical limit, we are forced to say that either the orderliness of the universe, which provides the necessary conditions that enable natural science, has no explanation or that it has an extra-natural one."[2]

Which of these alternatives is true is debatable, but the alternative itself is not. The quest for the ultimate basis of cosmic order reaches a dead end if natural science, which is explanation in terms of initial physical conditions and covering laws, is the only valid sort of rational explanation but whose own necessary conditions are, for whatever reason or lack of reason, unknowable or nonexistent.

It might perhaps be argued that, although the ultimate basis of cosmic order cannot be explained by natural science (in which this order is a logical precondition), it could perhaps be explained by some sort of philosophical but nontheistic argument. For example, somebody might reject the prevailing scientific materialism that seeks to explain reductively all phenomena, including organic life and human intelligence, in terms of basic but inexplicable laws of physics and chemistry. Instead she might, as we noted in a previous chapter, argue that there is an inherent, purely natural,

2. Haldane, "Philosophy Lives," 43.

94

and goal-directed purpose or teleology that underpins and explains the cosmic order and its basic scientific laws. This argument would claim that the scientifically intelligible orderliness of the universe and its temporal evolution are governed by an intrinsic purpose or goal—namely, the realization or actualization of a realm of meaning and value. This animating goal, it might be argued, is concretely achieved with the attainment or realization of its highest stage of development—namely, the evolved reality of human beings.

Such a claim would be the affirmation of a cosmic goal-driven evolution, tending towards a purposeful outcome to be achieved naturally without recourse to a divine designer. It would claim that the existence and recognition of value is not just a happy accidental evolutionary outcome. On the contrary, the existence and recognition of value is the intrinsic attracting goal and the ultimate explanation of the whole evolutionary process, most notably of the appearance of life with all its possibilities of development and variation.

Such an approach was intimated by Aristotle and continues to be argued and defended as the most satisfactory explanation of the orderliness of nature. It might be seen as a form of secularized Hegelianism. As I have indicated in the discussion of scientific naturalism in chapter 2, this approach is entertained as a serious possibility by the American philosopher Thomas Nagel. In his influential book, *Mind and Cosmos: Why the Materialist Neo-Darwinian Conception of Nature Is Almost Certainly False*, he writes:

But even though natural selection partly determines the details of the forms of life and consciousness that exist, and the relations among them, the existence of genetic material and the possible forms it makes available for selection have to be explained in some other way. The teleological hypothesis is that these things may be determined not merely by value-free chemistry and physics but also by something else, namely a cosmic predisposition to the formation of life, consciousness, and the value that is inseparable from them.[3]

Such an approach, which claims that the recognition and affirmation of value is the intrinsic purpose or goal of the order and development of the universe, is a more sophisticated and philosophically more adequate explanation than the reductive materialism suggested by exclusive reliance upon natural science. It gives due recognition to the intrinsic novelty and irreducibly emergent character of phenomena such as life, consciousness, and both theoretical and practical reason. It acknowledges what, more metaphysically, is called the analogy of being—the recognition that reality is characterized by different degrees or levels of being that are neither reducible to nor deducible from the physical components from which they are emergent.

However, this account of the universe in terms of a natural intrinsic value-driven goal or purpose is itself ultimately unintelligible if there is no further explanation of how or why this is so. For surely it is reasonable to wonder why such a seemingly inexplicable teleological or purposeful goal, about which it is claimed nothing further can be said, actually obtains. Such a goal may indeed provide an intelligible account of the necessary conditions for the nature and historical development of the universe as we know it. However, inasmuch as this goal itself is not self-explanatory, the question of its own necessary conditions presents itself. If these are unknown, unknowable, or nonexistent, the universe, for us, remains ultimately inexplicable.

Exclusive reliance on a groundless purpose that is not self-

3. Nagel, *Mind and Cosmos*, 123.

explanatory leads one to the same conclusion as exclusive reliance upon natural science, although admittedly in more sophisticated philosophical terminology. This conclusion states that the universe, however internally intelligible in terms of the evolutionary attainment of some natural goal or purpose, provides no ultimate philosophical explanation of how or why this is so. Does one have to be content to simply say that this is how, inexplicably, things happen to be?

Theistic arguments based upon such teleological considerations maintain that the necessary condition of the purposeful or goal-driven activity characteristic of the evolved universe can be discovered by us through indirect metaphysical argument. The teleologically formulated understanding of the universe as a purposeful goal-driven reality is ultimately explained by the affirmation of God as its self-explanatory transcendent intelligent creator.

In general terms, teleological explanation invokes the goal for the sake of which something occurs to account for its occurrence. Thus, a heart exists to serve the goal of sustaining the life of an organism by pumping its blood. The medical science of pathology pays indirect tribute to such teleological thinking. Similarly, as I have indicated, the human recognition and affirmation of objective rational values, both theoretical and practical, may be invoked as the goal that constitutes an explanation of the nature and development of the universe up to and including the emergence of human life. This development can now be understood as the orderly progressive advance towards the achievement and actual recognition of these values.

Since the remarkable growth of modern science, such teleological explanation is often dismissed as invoking *the concealed existence* of an unverifiable entity—namely, the alleged explanatory goal of the natural development of the universe. This rejection insists that genuine scientific explanation should be formulated exclusively in terms of empirically verifiable antecedent efficient causation. Such explanation identifies an empirically verifiable and antecedently existing cause of what is to be explained. A spider doesn't spin a web in order to catch flies. It catches flies because it is naturally and antecedently capable of spinning a web in which flies can be caught (if they exist in the web's environment). A duck doesn't have webbed feet in order to swim. It swims because it has naturally webbed feet. The basically physical universe has not evolved in order to attain the recognition and affirmation of objective values. It attains this recognition and affirmation because it has evolved physically from antecedent initial physical conditions by accidental mutation and natural selection. A theistic philosopher who argues teleologically must engage effectively with such significant objections about the unverifiable existence of the alleged goal and with the hugely successful replacement of teleological or final causation with the more empirically verifiable explanation of natural phenomena in terms of antecedent efficient causation.

First, the dismissive claim of modern science that teleological argument affirms the antecedent existence of an unverifiable entity—namely, the alleged goal—involves a serious misunderstanding. It loses sight of the paradoxical point that *the goal has no natural or self-possessed existence*, independent of our envisaging it, until it is effectively attained and realized—for example, by the actual snaring of the fly in the web, the actual swimming of the duck, or the actual recognition and affirmation of objective values. The real question to be addressed is how anything that does not yet have any mind-independent natural existence can explain, as its goal, purpose, or final cause, the occurrence of phenomena such as web-weaving spiders, web-footed ducks, or the evolution of human rationality.

Moreover, one can question the alleged scientific axiom that efficient causation has entirely eliminated and replaced any teleological speculation about a hypothetical yet-to-be-actualized final cause or goal. The two forms of explanation are not mutually incompatible and indeed can be usefully viewed as complementary. Each may provide us with reliable objective knowledge. The difference might be described by saying that in appealing to efficient causation we have explanation of a formal outcome (a duck swimming) in terms of antecedent function (possession of webbed feet) and that in appealing to final causation we have explanation of an antecedent function (possession of webbed feet) in terms of formal outcome (a duck swimming). There is no reason why both types of explanation cannot be availed of as useful, compatible, and mutually complementary. Thus, for example, we can validly claim both that veins have valves *in order* that blood can flow to the heart and that blood flows to the heart *because* veins have valves. As Peter Geach remarks, "'A happened in order that B should' is in nowise in conflict with 'B happened because A did.'"[4]

However, just as scientific explanation in terms of the orderly behavior of fundamental particles and the covering laws under which they operate cannot be used to explain these factors themselves, which are preconditions of this scientific explanation, a similar difficulty presents itself with teleological explanation. As indicated above, a teleological explanation of cosmic development exclusively in terms of this development's own attracting goal or outcome is, if considered only in itself, ultimately inexplicable and unintelligible. How can what as yet has no natural existence explain

4. Peter Geach, *Reason and Argument* (Oxford: Oxford University Press, 1976), 86.

anything? Such an inexplicable and nonexistent goal or purpose is unacceptable to both proponents and critics of teleology. Such a goal must, it is generally agreed, be explained either through replacement by a reductive materialist explanation in mechanistic terms or by some other consideration.

However, this dilemma cannot be resolved by appeal to a reductive mechanistic explanation. For, as we have already noted, any such reductive mechanistic explanation of phenomena is, if considered simply in itself, an ultimately inexplicable contingent datum. Consequently, the immanent teleology or goal orientation adduced to explain the internal intelligibility of the universe would, in such a reductive analysis, be shown to be a proximate internal explanation that is itself without any ultimate explanation. Unless some further consideration can be adduced, the internal intelligibility of the universe, whether described teleologically or more reductively in purely mechanistic terms, remains an unintelligible contingent fact. Let me suggest briefly why it is rationally incoherent to maintain both that the world is intrinsically intelligible, as the exercise of empirical science presupposes and affirms, and that this is ultimately a contingent and unintelligible brute fact.

We readily affirm the intrinsic intelligibility of the universe both in theory and in practice. For example, in a theoretical context we readily accept the objective validity of the laws of physics and chemistry, and in a practical context we habitually refrain from walking off cliffs or drinking poison. We acknowledge the enduring transfactual reality of a law-like universality and necessity vis-à-vis the merely factual and contingent features of experience. We view the factual interactions of material bodies that happen to constitute the universe as manifestations of causal powers and liabilities ("act and potency" in more traditional terminology) whose operation can be expressed scientifically in universal necessary laws. The touchstone of our scientific and metaphysical theorizing is our assured conviction about the intrinsic intelligibility of an independently existing world. This contention—that events in the world are rooted in a transfactual domain of law-like generative mechanisms of nature—contests Hume's view that the sequence of events can never be said to be more than an inexplicable conjunction of unconnected factual contingencies.

But if the law-like causal intelligibility of things is itself merely an inexplicable factual contingency, then it is difficult, in the ultimate analysis, to resist Hume's position. For if the enduring transfactual law-like intelligibility of things is itself a groundless factual contingency, then the ontological dependability and force of this causal law-like transcendence is undermined. The claims of Humean empiricism reaffirm themselves with a knock-on effect throughout the domain of intelligible experience. If the contrary of every contingent state of affairs is really possible, and if the law-like intelligibility of things ascribed to things just happens groundlessly and contingently to be the case, then we have no rational basis for the claim that such law-like intelligibility has always held good in the past or shall continue to do so in the future. Even if it has always held good in the past, that is no guarantee that it will do so in the future—any more than the chicken having been fed every day by the farmer is thereby assured that its neck will not be wrung by him on the morrow! If Hume's claim that there are no necessary connections between matters of fact is initially challenged by the evidence of law-like intelligibility, it is ultimately reaffirmed by the acceptance of the inexplicable contingent factuality of this law-like intelligibility itself.

But we do accept the contingent factuality of the intelligible world of our experience. That this particular world should exist—comprising the exact matter, energy, and intelligibility that it does—seems in no way necessary or inevitable. Hence we seem to be involved in an ontological dilemma. The inherent necessity and law-like intelligibility of the world, which we affirm as the preconditions of the universal laws of scientific achievement, are undermined and even contradicted by the claim that, considered simply in themselves, this necessity and intelligibility are ultimately only contingent facts. Can this dilemma be resolved without denying either the intrinsic law-like intelligibility of the world or its ultimate contingent factuality?

It can if we affirm that this contingent factuality is ultimately not an *inexplicable* brute fact but rather one freely and intelligently ordained by the purposeful creative decision of God. The intellectually conflicted affirmation—asserting (1) the intrinsically lawlike intelligibility and apparently teleological nature of the world and (2) its seemingly ultimate contingent factuality—urges theistic philosophers to pursue an ultimate explanation in terms of the conscious intention or design by God, envisaged as the transcendent creator of the universe and of its teleological development. Let me illustrate how such an ultimate theistic explanation might be proposed.

We are all aware of ourselves as agents who, by intention and design, initiate goal-directed activities and construct objects that operate in a manner that fulfills some purpose or goal. Such intentional activity can have either ourselves or something external to us as its object. Thus we decide to walk along the beach in order to personally enjoy the sea air. Or we can construct a fridge in order to keep food cool, a central heating system to maintain an equable room temperature, a power station to provide a community with energy. Our technological achievements can be validly considered as investing aspects of the physical universe with new purpose and significance.

Extrapolating from such lived experience of personally designed and achieved teleological effects, we can raise a further question. Does the universe that we inhabit and that manifests—in its dimensions of life, consciousness, and rationality—immanent teleological characteristics and objectives, such as the recognition and affirmation of truths and values, ultimately need to be understood as the intentionally designed creation of a transcendent personal creator?

The immanent teleological characteristic that I wish to consider in particular is human rationality in its theoretical and practical quest for meaning and value. I want to pursue a line of philosophical inquiry that is more basic than the various particular and limited realms of scientific inquiry disclosed by our cognitive openness to the world and to other people. Such basic philosophical interrogation of reality makes this world of lived experience and specialized scientific inquiry an object of further and more fundamental reflection. It is an interrogation that seeks some comprehension, however indirect, of how this extra-mental world and our cognitive experience and understanding of it can themselves have come to obtain and function together so remarkably. The interrogation seeks an account of how they have emerged and are co-constituted to present themselves as they do—as an independently intelligible universe "intentionally" or cognitively accessible to our finite minds or subjectivity.

The issue is how we, finite contingent organisms who are part of the physical world, can exist as self-conscious rational subjects to whose consciousness the independent objective intelligibility of this natural world is, to some extent at least, accessible. The puzzling question is how this world of which we are a part can be present to us as intelligibly given to our consciousness. As Edmund Husserl put it, "Can we be satisfied simply with the notion that human beings are *subjects for the world* (the world which for consciousness is their world) and at the same times are objects in this world? ... The juxtaposition 'subjectivity *in* the world as object' and at the same time 'conscious subject *for* the world' contains a necessary theoretical question, that of understanding how this is possible."[5]

Thomas Nagel has argued convincingly that even if a remarkable Darwinian organic evolution of occasionally mutating law-governed physical particles is a necessary condition for the emergence of this state of affairs, such organic evolution does not explain the irreducibly first-person dimension of rational subjectivity to which the objective intelligibility of the world is rendered accessible. It is in addressing this issue that explanation in terms of the purpose of a provident creator suggests itself.

How are we to understand and make rational sense of the undeniable state of affairs that, to a genuine if limited extent, the intrinsic intelligibility of an independently existing world is cognitively accessible to a part of that world—namely, our finite minds? As we have seen, a materialist mechanistic explanation—which would claim that the state of affairs is an inexplicable brute fact that has arisen simply through the accidental mutation of a law-like physical process— fails to address the complexity of the actual issue. What must be addressed is how an independent "third-person" world and our finite "first-person" minds have come to be and to

5. Edmund Husserl, *The Crisis of European Sciences and Transcendental Phenomenology*, trans. David Carr (Evanston, Ill.: Northwestern University Press, 1970), 180–81.

be so coordinated and interrelated that the independently existing intelligibility of the former is naturally accessible to the latter. This purposeful or goal-accomplishing state of affairs cries out for some account of how it can have come to be so.

How can it be that our minds and the independently existing world that we experience have evolved and are organized and ordered to enable us to realize (in the dual sense of make known and make real or actual) a specific teleological purpose or goal? This purpose or goal is the rational recognition and comprehension of the intelligibility of the world and of the objective values that it provides access to. We humans undoubtedly act purposively—that is, we discover truth through the exercise of our theoretical reason and effectively affirm value through the exercise of our practical reason. How can this be explained?

Nothing can be the adequate cause or explanation of something intrinsically independent of it. For this would involve the contradiction that the object envisaged both is and is not independent of its cause or explanation. But according to epistemological realism, our cognitive ability achieves knowledge or intentional understanding of the intelligible structures of a world that exists independently of our knowledge of it. An idealist account that wholly absorbs what is known within the knower is thereby precluded. What is known is not simply an effect of or an object constituted by our cognitive activity. It is something that intrinsically has a genuine independent intelligibility and transcendence vis-à-vis this cognitive activity. The sun's gravitational field obeys an inverse square law. Mount Everest is the highest mountain irrespective of our affirmation of that fact. That such things are so is not something that we invent or simply represent to ourselves. We discover it.

Realist philosophy claims that intelligible extra-mental being, although attained by our knowledge, reveals itself, in its very signification, as not dependent upon the cognitive act that grasps it. The existence and intelligibility of what we know are irreducible to being known either actually or potentially by the human spirit. Our understanding of an object's activity is really dependent upon and affected by the object known. But what is known is not similarly dependent upon or affected by our knowing. The relationship between our knowing and what we know is an asymmetrical one in which only one term of the relationship is modified. Instead of seeking unavailingly to explain this cognitive relationship in exclusively materialist or idealist terms or of simply accepting it as an inexplicable brute fact, let us consider whether and how a different explanation that accounts for its purposeful character can be argued.

This alternative explanation interprets this purposeful goal-achieving state of affairs in terms of the intentional design of an intelligent agent. In other words, the purposeful or teleological fit between our minds and extra-mental reality that obtains *in order that* we may achieve the specific goods of having reliable knowledge and recognizing objective values implies a purposeful creator.

According to the teleological explanation, *the specifying good to be achieved* through the purposeful and dependable fit or coordination of our minds with extra-mental reality—namely, reliable human knowledge of extra-mental reality—*does not yet exist* prior to the purposeful fit that accomplishes it. Such an explanation, which is essentially an explanation in terms of a good or beneficial result to be achieved, differs from Darwinian naturalistic explanation, which also involves a reference to what is good or beneficial. This latter explanation explains how a particular outcome (e.g., a better-adapted species) is produced *as a result* of a good or beneficial accidental mutation of initial conditions that has already naturally occurred and that, when combined with the consequent mechanism of natural selection, produces the better-adapted species. Teleological explanation, on the contrary, "explains" the anterior circumstances and structures (e.g., the felicitous harmony of mind and reality) by reference to a *yet to be achieved* good outcome.

But this poses the formidable question: how can this purposeful fit be explained by a goal that, as yet, has no concretely achieved natural existence? In the search to resolve this genuine difficulty, the move from a discussion of purpose or teleology to a discussion of design arises with the claim that the difficulty can be met if the specifying good preexists in the mind of a purposeful creator capable of creating the conditions necessary for the good's realization.[6] Our own immanent intelligence cannot be the adequate source of this purposeful creation since the existence and exercise of this intelligence presuppose the goal—namely, reliable human knowledge of extra-mental reality, which the ordered relationship between our intelligence and an independently existing world accomplishes.

We are drawn to envisage an adequate and purposeful creator as causing to exist and be, such as they are, both the intelligible extra-mental world and our ability to understand it—and also the asymmetrical nonmutual relationship in which they stand to one another. Such an account would provide an ultimate rationale of a teleological account of our objective knowledge in a way that a naturalistic account exclusively in terms of inexplicable and irreducible purpose cannot. The intellectually unsatisfactory hypothesis of irreducible natural purpose suggests either a reductive materi-

6. Anthony Kenny, "The Argument from Design," in *Reason and Religion: Essays in Philosophical Theology* (Oxford: Blackwell, 1987), 69–84.

alist mechanistic explanation, which I have argued is intrinsically problematic, or an account in theistic terms of God's purposeful creation, which I suggest provides an adequate explanation.

We have an analogue for such a theistic explanation in terms of divine design in our experience of the existence of any contingent but not naturally occurring ordered teleological system—for example, a thermostat or a refrigerator. Such a system is accounted for in terms of human intelligence freely deciding to devote activity to the realization of this system rather than to some other contingent possibility. In an analogous way, the naturally occurring but not naturalistically or mechanistically explicable orderly fit of our contingent minds with the extra-mental intelligibility of the physical world is accounted for by the affirmation of a divine creative intelligence. The free decision of this creative intelligence brings into being the necessary conditions for this contingent but remarkable state of affairs.

The analogy holds good because in each case a contingently coordinated or orderly state of affairs occurs that finds its requisite explanation in terms of a freely designed decision of an intelligent agent. However, it is only an analogy because there are also distinctive differences between the two cases, notwithstanding their similarities. The human agent, like any finite agent, is itself contingent, and the artificial teleological order that it establishes presupposes the existence of the contingent natural intelligibility of the world. The divine agent, on the other hand, exists noncontingently and freely causes to exist, *ex nihilo*, both the contingent intelligible universe to which we belong and our rational ability to understand, at least to some extent, the universe's objective extra-mental intelligible structure.

God does not require similar explanation because he is affirmed as existing independently of the contingent natural order, which he is invoked to explain—that is, he exists noncontingently or necessarily and hence as self-explanatory. In summary, we affirm the existence of God as the intelligent source that makes sense of our account of our objective knowledge in terms of the teleologically understood harmony between our finite minds and the natural world.

The line of argument indicated above does not depend upon Leibniz's grandiose and dubious principle according to which our understanding of the intelligibility of the natural world requires the existence of God as the sufficient reason why the world must exist and exist thus and not otherwise. It relies rather on the more modest claim that this contingent state of affairs would be incoherent or contradictory in the absence of an intelligent creator who exists necessarily and self-sufficiently. In other words, I suggest that the fundamental metaphysical principle operative in the metaphysical argument for the existence of God is not the principle of sufficient reason but rather the principle of noncontradiction. The argument seeks to show that the state of affairs that we have been considering requires, in the ultimate analysis, the affirmation of God as its creative cause if we are to avoid incompatible and contradictory affirmations about it. These would be affirmations such as "Our claim to objective knowledge of the world is reliable" and "Our claim to objective knowledge of the world has no reliable ultimate explanation."

The foregoing discussion illustrates how an argument for the existence of God can be developed from the nonmutual relationship of dependence involved in our ability to understand the intelligible structure of the extra-mental world. This paradoxical relationship is a cipher within experience of the analogous relationship of nonmutual real dependence of the world upon God. It serves as an illuminating source of argument from a "transcendence" manifest within our cognitive experience to the "beyond-experience-ness" of the absolute transcendent God.

The nonmutual relationship between our knowledge and the world is like a mirror image of the relationship between the world and God. It is a relationship that enables a "reflection" from a humanly experienced asymmetry to the ultimate asymmetry that is the relationship between God and the world. The similarity of the relationship was noted succinctly by Aquinas, who writes: "Now the relation which God is said to bear to creatures, though represented mentally as existing in God, exists not in God but in the creatures, just as things are called objects of knowledge not because they are related to knowledge, but because knowledge is related to them."[7]

7. Aquinas, *Summa theologiae* I q. 6, art. 2, ad 1.

Seven

"ONLY BY LOVE"—ANOTHER APPROACH

Undoubtedly a metaphysical argument for the existence of God, such as that outlined in the previous chapter, will not be universally convincing. It will not, for example, commend itself to the intellectual mindset of scientific naturalists or humanists, who are committed to an exclusively empirical or secular framework of theoretical inquiry and who methodologically reject any appeal to the sort of teleological explanation that the particular metaphysical argument I outlined employs.

Nor does such a metaphysical argument automatically engender a commitment to religious belief and worship on the part of everyone who is prepared to concede it some rational plausibility. The God disclosed by metaphysical reasoning is often and explicitly rejected, even by some religious believers, in the name of human freedom, autonomy, or even authentic religious belief. The creature–creator relationship characteristic of the abstract impersonal metaphysical argument is often perceived as yielding only a limited, dehumanized, and servile conception of the human condition and of its relationship to God. That is to say, such a relationship is perceived as an inherently inadequate account of the God–humanity relationship. Such rejection of a metaphysical account of God is explicitly and emphatically asserted in most of the discussions in Richard Kearney's interesting book *Reimagining the Sacred* mentioned in the previous chapters.

Religious believers (like myself) who insist that metaphysical claims are important may be asked how to respond. It can be readily admitted that the metaphysical argument is indeed a limited representation of the human–divine relationship and that the argument makes no claim to generate any profound religious commitment. However, I would claim that its account, however limited, is a true and important account of how ultimate reality must be conceived from a nonreligious, strictly philosophical viewpoint. And the metaphysical argument does raise, even if it does not resolve, some unavoidable issues about religious belief and worship. The recognition of oneself as created does have some logically self-involving consequences—even if only the posing of the issue of one's response to this situation.

In this chapter I would like to consider how such an externally based abstract and objective metaphysical argument for the existence of God might be complemented by more internally based and subject-centered considerations. I wish to explore whether the objective metaphysical conclusion that God exists might be complemented by an equally reasonable but more personally involved commitment to his existence. This reflection is inspired by Saint Augustine's striking declaration that "Only through love can one enter into truth" ("Non intratur in veritatem nisi per caritatem").[1]

Instead of proceeding from an objective affirmation of God as provident creator (attained through faith or as the conclusion of an objective metaphysical argument) and advancing on that basis, by way of rational hope, to love and worship of the God thus objectively

1. Augustine, *Contra Faustum* 41, 32, 18; PL 45, 507.

affirmed, I propose to pursue a reversal of this cognitive itinerary. I will consider how one may proceed from a self-involving love of God—envisaged indirectly as a totally adequate object of desire—by way of a rationally articulated hope to a confident and assured affirmation of his reality. I will seek to argue for the reasonability of my love of and desire for God—God precisely envisaged indirectly as infinite goodness, as the metaphysical argument would claim. This desire is not just another illusory aspiration but one inspired by an experiential intimation or cipher of an objective reality; I will show God to be a reality in whom I have good reason to hope and consequently to whom I can confidently pledge my absolute commitment.

In general terms, it can be said that we love or desire what we envisage or understand to be good or of value. I must believe whatever I honestly call good or of value to be so independently of my simply desiring or loving it. A genuine good is not a mere expression of my desires and wishes; rather, it is an objective value whose role is to order and motivate these desires and wishes appropriately in accordance with how things, including my human nature, really are. My desire is relative to what is good—not it to my desire.

However, it is necessary to explain that this does not mean I am always right in representing the objective good or value to myself. It does not follow that whatever we effectively desire is therefore always really or objectively good—even though we may so represent it to ourselves. Thus, for example, we can in certain circumstances tell ourselves that adultery or robbery or even murder is necessary to attain a good or is even good in itself. Aroused by passion or blinded by selfishness, such immoral deeds can indeed be represented illusorily as desirable goods to be attained even though they cannot be judged impersonally and objectively to be so. The challenge, then, is to distinguish between desires that are only apparently good and desires that are genuine, both by purifying ourselves from passion and selfishness and by attending to what is real. What I aim to argue here is that my loving desire for God, who is envisaged as infinite goodness, is not just a childish illusion or an exercise in wish fulfillment but an objectively motivated aspiration for a good in which I have genuine reason to hope and consequently to rationally affirm.

But this argument immediately runs into the trouble of defining what it is about. Many would deny that they have any such desire for God. Logical positivists will dismiss it as a meaningless exercise in wish fulfillment, and secular Marxists will speak derisively of a placating, deceptive hope for "pie in the sky when you die." For committed atheists, such as many humanists and scientists, talk of love or desire for God, far from being a noble ideal, is a symptom of human alienation. Our love and desires, they insist, should remain contained within the limitations of our finite condition and the intrinsic possibilities of the natural universe.

Moreover, the ambiguity and capacity for self-deception inherent in our conceptions of "love" and "good" affect our discernment and appraisal of the desires and activities that should be cultivated as conducive to genuine human fulfillment. Hence it is not surprising that various sophisticated philosophical accounts about what constitutes human flourishing (to say nothing of popular understandings or television advertisements) leave out the desire for a relationship with God altogether. In engaging with such proponents of an exclusively secular viewpoint, it may be more appropriate to initiate the conversation with a discussion of the more generally agreed-upon human desire for happiness.

Perhaps it can be shown that the desire for God is implicit, but initially unrecognized, in our generally accepted desire for happiness. As Thomas Aquinas remarks, "Now, man naturally desires God in so far as he naturally desires happiness which is a certain likeness of the divine goodness. On this basis it is not necessary that God considered in Himself be naturally known to man, but only a likeness of God."[2] Or as Saint Augustine expressed it more personally in his *Confessions*, "Thou hast made us for thyself O Lord and our hearts are restless until they rest in thee."

In our desire for happiness, we long to possess and enjoy the goods or values that constitute a dependable realization and fulfillment of our specifically human nature and aspirations. Other beings move to their specific fulfillment in a determined and necessitated manner. They are not free to perform actions incompatible with their specific natures. An apple tree, for example, has no option in the matter of growing, blossoming, and bearing fruit in due season (although external circumstance, such as a prolonged frost, may frustrate this predetermined fulfillment of its specific nature). At the human level, however, we encounter a level of reality that is intelligent and free and that can pursue fulfillment and happiness in a rational, voluntary, and loving manner. This pursuit must discern for itself the sort of values and the corresponding appropriate loving desires and aspirations that must be cultivated as conducive to this fulfillment and happiness.

Aristotle was one of the early philosophers who devoted attention to discerning the true nature of human happiness. In his *Nicomachean Ethics*, he develops an account of happiness as living in accordance with the habitual exercise of the best and most perfect virtue—namely, the intellectual virtue of speculative contemplation

2. Aquinas, *Summa contra Gentiles* I, ch. 3.

of truth, goodness, and beauty, exercised in agreeable circumstances, in the company of good friends, and enduring unto old age.

This is undoubtedly a benign and lofty conception of a life that is desirable, lovable, and worthy of pursuit in order to attain our specifically human goal of happiness! Even though it involves no explicit reference to a desire for God, it comes close with its concentration upon the importance of personal reflection on the close association between genuine happiness and a virtuous life governed by practical concern for ultimate truth, goodness, and beauty. Although not everyone may enjoy the happy circumstance envisaged by Aristotle, his conception provides a perceptive indication of the close association between genuine happiness and a virtuous life governed by respect for the requirements of truth, goodness, and beauty.

However, Aristotle is realist enough to acknowledge a major challenge to this conception of human happiness. Can a man be happy if he experiences great misfortune? Can he, for example, be happy if he experiences the suffering of Priam grieving over the death of his beloved son Hector? Aristotle suggests that in such a predicament a good person will not be happy, although he may continue to act virtuously. Aristotle would have endorsed his compatriot Solon's lament: "Call no man happy until he is dead." Aristotle's appreciation of the fragility of happiness and of the ambiguity of the relationship between virtue and happiness enables us to revisit these issues briefly in more contemporary idiom.

Our love and desire for happiness is not fulfilled automatically. It must seek its fulfillment by the free exercise of our distinguishing feature—our reason. We differ most significantly from other inhabitants of the animal world through our freedom and our intellectual capacity to reason appropriately and to discern for ourselves the prerequisites of our happiness. In considering what is involved in such an appropriate exercise of reason, we sometimes get into a muddle because we adopt too restricted a view of what is meant by "reason" or "rationality." We tend to think of it exclusively in logical terms as primarily an activity of drawing irresistible conclusions from self-evident propositions, as in mathematics, or of deducing universal but impersonal physical laws out of messy experimental data, as in modern science. Such conceptions of reason have very limited existential significance, which is why living according to "reason alone" is so seldom practiced or desired. We can, however, take a more positive approach to reason's importance to our lives if we embrace a more comprehensive view of reason: a view that sees reason as a liberating capacity that enables us to live in a specifically human way with a rational openness—to the world, to other people, to ourselves, and possibly even to God.

The light of reason opens us beyond our bodily limitations to participate in a life of scientific enquiry and cultural achievement. We can progress from knowing particular truths to knowing scientific laws and theories and, finally, to marveling and wondering at our experience of the intelligibility, truthfulness, and alluring beauty of reality that grounds our scientific endeavors. It is indeed remarkable that through us the material universe, of which we are an integral component, can come to know itself, discover the domain of values, and ponder its own and our ultimate meaning and value.

Likewise, in the practical sphere, reason enables us to apply our scientific knowledge to participate in and contribute to a world of technological marvels. It also qualifies us to act in a manner that enables us to develop from mere instinctual self-interest, through mild benevolence, to ethical acknowledgment of the absolute moral demands that another person can make on us. We can even come to love another person selflessly through loving her intrinsic and more than simply physical excellence and goodness. Again, we can marvel at the various levels of rational questions we can put to *ourselves* in seeking to understand ourselves. As Kant observed, reason enables us to ask: "What can we know?" "What should we do?" and "For what may we hope?"—each level involving its own type of rational discourse.

In a word, through the life of reason we can come to live under the authority of values such as truth, beauty, justice, goodness, and love. I believe that both theists and atheists can agree about this conception of an authentic human life governed by these requirements of reason and about its consonance with our natural desire for happiness. They can cooperate in promoting this conception of an authentic life, whatever its ultimate significance and value.

Although an affirmation of the existence of God is not a logical or epistemological presupposition of this conception of the life of reason, the hope or desire that he may indeed exist is not irrational or irrelevant to such a conception. For such hope in his existence as a personal creative principle of unrestricted truth, beauty, justice, goodness, and love would make ultimate and dependable sense of this conception of the life of reason in a way that atheism does not. For this hope grounds and validates these values (which are the lifeblood of human reason) as most ultimately real, dependable, and non-transitory.

This hope can be viewed as an aspirational but not irrational personal response to the impersonal physical second law of thermodynamics, which, in its affirmation of the principle of entropy, proclaims a cosmic tendency to ultimate disorder, randomness, and chaos. This affirmation of universal entropy can be qualified by a hopeful commitment to the countervailing principle of negative entropy, affirmed as recognition of the order-creating capacity of reason and love. Such commitment to the principle of negative entropy, formulated originally by the scientist Erwin Schrödinger, can be developed as an argument that ultimately the characteristic order-attaining capacity of our reason and love implies, requires, or is congruent with an affirmation of God as a more fundamental reality than the cosmic tendency to randomness, disorder, and chaos signaled by the physical principle of entropy. Our reason and love, apprehended as order-generating energy capable of achieving and promoting truth, goodness, and beauty, can engender a rational hope that this promotion of desirable order is ultimately vindicated by the reality of God—affirmed as infinite truth, goodness, and beauty transcending the disorder of material contingency, randomness, mindlessness, and ultimate chaos predicted by physical science.

Atheism, on the other hand, is committed, I think, to judging that these values of reason and love, however uncompromisingly and heroically affirmed, not only are eventually and inevitably eliminated by death for each individual but also, and more fundamentally, are destined to ultimate and total extinction within an inescapable context of contingency, chaos, and inexplicable brute fact. These values are disclosed as neither necessarily obtaining nor ultimately vindicated. They just happen to have occurred or evolved accidentally and inexplicably and are destined, as empirical science predicts, to peter out in a silent inanimate universe. As Bertrand Russell puts it, "All the labors of the ages, all the devotion, all the inspiration, all the noonday brightness of human genius are destined to extinction in the vast death of the solar system."[3]

3. Bertrand Russell, "A Free Man's Worship," in *Mysticism and Logic and Other Essays* (London: George Allen and Unwin, 1917), 37–38.

If human intelligence and freedom—and their capacity to recognize values such as truth goodness, beauty, and love—owe their ultimate origin and significance either to an infinite intelligent and free creator or to a chance and radically contingent modification of the configuration of mindless matter, it seems odd to use that same intelligence and freedom to choose the latter rather than the former as a more reasonable explanation of their reality. It seems a profound irony to claim that one of the most significant achievements of human rationality is to prove its own ultimate insignificance and the ultimate triumph of entropy!

Indeed, it can even be claimed that the attempt to argue rationally that the defining values of rational discourse are ultimately inexplicable, unintelligible, and contingent modifications of mindless matter involves a performative contradiction. For it would certainly seem that the formulation of the argument contradicts its conclusion. The argument, which concludes that ultimately truth and goodness are contingent phenomena and that reality is ultimately devoid of rational significance, depends for its alleged validity on the more fundamental reliability of such rational argumentation itself. It is comparable to an argument that all logical reasoning is invalid—an argument that involves a presupposed confidence in the performative efficacy of logical reasoning to make the claim.

The hopeful affirmation of God as an infinite personal source of dependable meaning and value is a profoundly self-involving affirmation, unlike the detached objective deliverances of mathematics, physics, or even metaphysics. It expresses a hopeful validation of a rational concern for meaning and value and a repudiation of the despairing suggestion that the life of reason and its defining activities, such as the attainment of truth, goodness, beauty, and love, originated mindlessly and are destined to perish in post-human mindless oblivion.

This is not to deny the remarkable commitment of atheists to a life devoted to the requirements of reason. Indeed, their commitment is all the more remarkable in that it seems to them that the fundamental nature of reality provides such requirements with no ultimate vindication—their commitment is a witness to the intrinsic value of truth, regardless of its ultimate significance. However, it does seem that our quest for happiness, envisaged as the dependable fulfillment of the loving desires of a life lived according to the theoretical and practical exigencies of reason, can, in its reasonable desire for confirmation and ultimate validation, rationally hope in the existence of a personal provident creator. Atheists, who also affirm that life should be lived rationally under the authority of truth and goodness, might concede that this personal provident creator, if such exists, would make ultimate sense of our rational aspirations, even though on other grounds they might reject this existence as delusional. They might be persuaded that the existential hope is reasonable because it makes ultimate and dependable sense of a rational conception of the good life in a way that their atheism, however heroic, cannot provide on the basis of their own conception of the ultimate nature of reality.

This reasonable hope in or desire for God is not logically undeniable, and it must address the objections that an atheist might pose to it. But neither is it just an exercise in self-delusion. Such hope is a genuinely rational way of envisaging the ultimate significance of reality in general and of human existence in particular. It envisages, as a rational *desideratum*, the real coincidence of what is inherently valuable with how things ultimately and fundamentally are. It maintains that it is reasonable to hope that reality is intrinsically valuable, ultimately characterized by values such as truth, goodness, beauty, and love rather than by contingent inexplicable occurrences, and it affirms the existence of a provident creator as the transcendent necessary condition of this being so. As Wittgenstein observes, "The sense of the world must lie outside the world. . . . If there is a value which is of value, it must lie outside all happening and being so. For all happening and being-so is accidental."[4]

It is surely reasonable to love the conception of oneself as participating in a universe characterized by life-enhancing rational values that are sustained and assured of ultimate significance by a provident personal creator. From this loving conception of a desirable state of affairs, one is naturally and reasonably attracted to hope that this is indeed how things are. And on the basis of this rational hope one can, in expressing a rational existential engagement, commit oneself to it being so. Based upon a loving desire for and a rational hope in the existence of God as provident creator of an ultimately intelligible and desirable universe, I can rationally engage myself to live my life as an existential commitment to this being how reality ultimately is.

Immanuel Kant, the philosopher who provided the most trenchant criticism of the traditional metaphysical arguments for the existence of God, provides a spirited defense of such an existential hope-based affirmation of God. In his philosophy, he finds a dependable foundation for an affirmation of God through rational faith based upon rational hope. Since he maintains that such rational faith is inaccessible by way of theoretical reason, this faith must belong to the rationality of practical knowledge in its formulation

---

4. Ludwig Wittgenstein, *Tractatus logico-philosophicus* (London: Routledge and Kegan Paul, 1922), 6.41.

of what is good or of value. He argues that it is through reflection upon reason, in its moral determination of the kind of activity that is good or of value, that one can come to an affirmation of the existence of God as a postulate or presupposition of morality.

When Kant speaks of God as a postulate of morality, he does not at all mean that belief in God is the basis or motivating principle of morality. On the contrary, he insists on the absolute autonomy of morality—what one ought to do is discovered, *sui generis*, by the rational person. Thus he affirms:

So far as morality is based upon the conception of man as a free agent who, just because he is free, binds himself through his reason to unconditioned laws, it stands in need neither of another Being over him, for him to apprehend his duty, nor of an incentive other than the law itself, for him to do his duty.... Hence for its own sake morality does not need religion at all (whether objectively, as regards willing, or subjectively, as regards ability [to act]; by virtue of pure practical reason it is self-sufficient.[5]

The existence of God is postulated by Kant in the context of practical reason not as the foundation of morality but as a condition of the due accomplishment and fulfillment of morality's rational exigencies. The moral law, which man imposes upon himself by his practical reason, directs him to seek an unconditioned object—namely, the *summum bonum* or highest good. Upon reflection, this object is seen to be a complex one. In the first place it involves the supreme and absolute condition of all moral action—namely, action that derives from a dutiful will or virtue. Our actions should always be motivated primarily by what we virtuously recognize to be our self-imposed and universally applicable duty. But as well as this

5. Immanuel Kant, *Religion within the Limits of Reason Alone*, trans. Theodore M. Greene and Hoyt H. Hudson (New York: Harper Torchbooks, 1960), 3.

necessary but insufficient condition of the *summum bonum*, the enjoyment of happiness in due proportion to virtue is also required. In Kant's estimation, the affirmation of God is required in order to ensure and even to render possible the necessary bond between these two components of the *summum bonum*.

Although the pursuit of happiness cannot be the decisive criterion of moral action for Kant, it is also true that to act morally or virtuously is to behave in such a manner as to be worthy or deserving of happiness. No appraisal of how a rational ordering of things would be could reasonably decide otherwise. "For to need happiness, to deserve it, and yet at the same time not to participate in it, cannot be consistent with the volition of a rational being."[6]

However, the ultimate coherence of this rational exigency or practical necessity that virtue should be accompanied by due happiness and thus accomplish the whole or perfect good (which the moral law bids us to promote) requires that God exist. Happiness depends upon the harmony of the course of nature with a person's wish and will. Since the human will cannot dictate the course of natural events, the necessary connection between virtue and happiness can be assured only through recourse to an infinite being, who alone can guarantee the ultimate accomplishment of a state of affairs in which happiness is exactly proportioned to virtue.

We ought to endeavor to promote the *summum bonum*, which, therefore, must be possible. Accordingly, the existence of a cause of all nature, distinct from nature itself, and containing the principle of this connection, namely, of the exact harmony of happiness with morality, is also postulated.... The supreme cause of nature, which must be presupposed as a

<hr/>

6. Immanuel Kant, *Critique of Practical Reason*, 6th ed., trans. Thomas K. Abbott (London: Longmans, 1909), 206.

condition of the *summum bonum*, is a being which is the cause of nature by *intelligence* and *will*, consequently its author, that is God.[7]

Thus Kant affirms the existence of God not as a speculative truth to resolve a metaphysical contradiction but rather as an existential truth to resolve a lived conflict and disproportion experienced by the ethical man between empirical happiness and the demands of duty. Given, as we have seen that Aristotle fully appreciated, that a life governed by unfailing commitment to the unconditional requirement of dutiful or virtuous behavior is not inevitably accompanied in experience by the happiness that is appropriate and due to such a virtuous life, man's expression of a rational hope and loving desire affirms the existence of an infinite God. This God is affirmed as one who can, in the fullness of time, affect a total reconciliation between virtue and happiness. "The righteous man may say: I *will* that there be a God, and that my existence in this world be also an existence outside the chain of physical events, and in a pure world of the understanding, and lastly, that my duration be endless."[8]

The trans-speculative and decidedly existential character of Kant's affirmation of God is highlighted by his insistence that it is inappropriate to impose the impersonal mode of discourse upon a statement of theistic certainty. The latter is essentially personal since my theistic conviction is drawn out of a concrete reflection upon my own subjectivity in its moral dimension. Thus Kant observes:

My conviction is not *logical* but *moral* certainty; and since it rests on subjective grounds (of moral sentiment), I must not even say, "*It is* morally

7. Ibid., 221–22.
8. Ibid., 241.

certain that there is a God etc.," but "*I am* morally certain, etc." In other words, belief in a God and another world is so interwoven with my moral sentiment that as there is little danger of my losing the latter, there is equally little cause to fear that the former can ever be taken from me.[9]

Kant's conviction is that loving commitment to a virtuous and duty-respecting life, and acknowledgment that happiness is this life's appropriate accompaniment, enables a rational hope (and thereby a personally assured belief) in the existence of God as the necessary condition of this specifically human commitment. It is an impressive example, particularly from someone so unconvinced by objective metaphysical argument, that there is an alternative rational approach to the existence of God: an approach moving from committed love of what is perceived to be the highest and most desirable moral good, through rational hope, to personal belief in the existence of God as the assured foundation of this *summum bonum*.

In a later chapter on our love of God, I will explore further this conviction that loving desire for the greatest good provides access to a practical affirmation of God, as distinct from a purely speculative one. I will consider how such conviction may find an echoing confirmation through a particular interpretation of St. Anselm's famous—indeed notorious—ontological argument for the existence of God. This argument claims that from our idea of God as the being than which none greater or better can be conceived, we can conclude directly to his existence in reality and not just as a concept in our mind. I will suggest that although quite unconvincing as an abstract metaphysical argument, it can be interpreted as an illuminating account of the ultimate significance of our loving desire for the true, the good, and the beautiful.

9. Kant, *Critique of Pure Reason*, trans. N. Kemp Smith (London: Macmillan, 1968), B857.

Eight

TOWARD A THEOLOGY
OF LOVE

In previous chapters I have considered various approaches to the
great background question of our conscious lives: "What does it all
ultimately mean?" I have considered various ideas proposed to answer this basic question. These included discussions of humanism,
scientism (and scientific naturalism), and philosophical theism.

Because theism provides the answer that I personally find most
convincing, I have devoted the most attention to it. I outlined various philosophical aspects of this theistic answer. I discussed the
relationship between philosophy and religious faith or belief. I
considered how both phenomenology and linguistic philosophy
seek, each in its own way, to offer a philosophical vindication of
theistic belief that rejects the traditional speculative metaphysical
approach of natural theology. These philosophies question the religious relevance and validity of such an approach, which seeks to
provide objective, theoretical arguments concerning the existence
and nature of God. They argue that the only viable philosophical
approach to God today is one that envisages him exclusively as
corresponding to our specifically human religious sentiments, requirements, and aspirations.

In response, I presented a defense of the speculative and objective metaphysical approach as at least a valid complementary approach. I did so by outlining a theoretical, metaphysical, teleological argument for the existence of God as the free intelligent creator of the orderly goal-achieving activity of the finite components of the universe, most notably ourselves. Finally, I considered another more practical, personal, and existential approach to an affirmation of the existence of God—an approach based on our loving desire for happiness and our rational hope in the reality of the goodness that would assure that happiness's attainability.

In the following chapters I wish to reflect further on the theistic response to the fundamental background question of our lives. I will seek to illustrate how the central conclusions of my theoretical and practical philosophical discussion are developed and then amplified by the theological perspective disclosed by Christian revelation. I will seek to illustrate how both the indirectly argued affirmation of a divine creator by theoretical metaphysical reasoning and the practical, rationally inspired, and hopeful commitment to the existence of a lovable and loving God are richly confirmed and amplified in Christian theology. That we are created by God and that we are loved by God are two central truths of Christianity— truths that Christian theology elucidates in terms that greatly surpass the intimations of these truths that philosophical reflection might otherwise attain.

Metaphysics, phenomenology, and theology are three different kinds of discourse, each of which seeks to provide dependable knowledge about God as the ultimate source of all meaning and value. They are each animated, one might say, by a distinct first principle or animating concept from which a coherent account of everything may be unfolded. These three principles are (1) "the objective affirmation of being" in metaphysics, (2) "the given to human consciousness" in phenomenology, and (3) "the word of God as revealed to faith" in theology.

Theology, broadly understood as the systematic exposition and ordering of truths revealed by God, dramatically exceeds the philosophical disclosures about God proposed by metaphysics and phenomenology (and its linguistic philosophy equivalent) and considered simply as products of natural reason. It enlarges and transforms what is anticipated by natural reason concerning the existence and nature of God as creator and infinitely lovable goodness.

From the earliest biblical revelation to the definitive declarations of the Councils of Nicaea and Constantinople, the Judeo-Christian God has been affirmed as "Creator of heaven and earth, of all things visible and invisible," existing "before all ages." This God is radically distinguished from all pagan affirmations and descriptions of gods. Unlike the gods of pagans or Gentiles, this God of Christian revelation and theology is not a part, not even the best part, of the world. Pagan gods originated within and as part of the world. The Christian God is the originator of the world, a world from which he is radically distinct and of which he is the creator. Moreover, he is not God only because he is creator. Creation depends upon God, not God upon creation. As Robert Sokolowski remarks:

God does not exist primarily as part of the world, nor does he exist primarily as Creator of the world (if he did, he would have to create in order to be as perfect as possible). The biblical God would be God even if the world had not been created. He would be no less perfect if he had not created. This understanding of God sheds light on what Creation is: it is an action done out of sheer generosity and goodness, with no need, no imperfection prompting it.[1]

---

1. Robert Sokolowski, *Christian Faith and Human Understanding* (Washington, D.C.: The Catholic University of America Press, 2006), 61.

The relationship between the world and God is one of creation and not, as Hegel maintained one of correlation.

The discussion of God in natural theology or metaphysics approximates to this biblical account of God as creator. By indirect metaphysical argument, such reflection claims to establish that God exists as the infinitely perfect creator of the finite universe from which he is absolutely independent as self-sufficient infinite perfection of existence. The biblical references to creation and their theological elaboration provide a much richer and humanly more significant development of this rational attainment of an objective metaphysical affirmation of God as creator of the finite universe.

Further, in its unfolding of the revelation of the Trinitarian character of God's life, theology provides profound knowledge about his divine nature and about its relevance to an account of the ultimate meaning and value of human existence. Such knowledge, although compatible with philosophical investigation, is entirely beyond the range of philosophical speculation. We are invited to meditate upon the nature of our one God, a knowing and loving God, truly distinguished in tri-personal terms as Father, Son, and Spirit—divine ultimate Being, Truth, and Goodness. Our theological affirmation of this Trinitarian God who is love constitutes the fundamental and ultimate context for our religious appreciation of the other great Christian mystery: the Incarnation, infinite God become finite man.

This astonishing revelation that God himself partook of human nature in the person of Jesus Christ (and this revelation's subsequent theological elaboration) discloses the most remarkable and wholly unforeseen relationship between human beings and their creator. If the theological account of the Trinitarian nature of God's life elucidates the revelation that the life of God is a life of infinite love, the theological account of the mystery of the Incarnation elucidates the revelation that we humans are, in a privileged way, recipients of and enabled to participate in this divine love. In order to try to throw some light upon this astonishing revelation of our enabled participation in God's love, I propose to take a detour to reflect upon the nature of our natural human love, a love that divine love transforms so remarkably.

In order to outline this understanding of human love and how God's love transforms it, I have recourse again to the concept of "emergence," which featured prominently in the critique of reductionist materialism in chapter 2. This concept also provides an illuminating perspective from which to consider the nature of our distinctive human capacity to love.

Nine

EMERGENCE

A reductionist and exclusively materialist understanding of human love, as fundamentally comparable to a fortuitous wave on the surface of the sea or to an electrochemical neural event, is implausible to anyone who loves. As an essentially first-person activity, love cannot be adequately described or explained in exclusively third-person terminology. I suggest that instead we should make recourse to the technical concept of "emergence."

"Emergence," as I indicated in chapter 2, refers to novel properties of a system or entity. A property is said to be emergent if it is a qualitatively new property of a system or entity that obtains at a certain level of complexity in that system or entity. An emergent property enables the entity to exercise a novel form of causality. Moreover, the novel property is neither deducible from nor reducible to the physical components or properties of the material entity in which it subsists and from which it is emergent.

This understanding of emergence as the realization of irreducible novelty is of considerable philosophical interest. For it poses a challenge to what has been called the prevailing scientific orthodoxy of reductionist materialism. The contention of this prevailing viewpoint is that a properly scientific explanation of any object of inquiry—including the origin of life, of consciousness, of reason and indeed of love itself—must be provided, or at least sought exclusively, in terms of a reductive account that ultimately avails itself only of the laws of physics and chemistry. Life and love come to be understood by analogy with the dead and are interpreted as fortunate but fortuitous accidents in an all-embracing, basically mechanical process.

Reflection on the idea of emergence, as establishing at various levels the realization of irreducibly novel efficacious properties, provides a context and perspective for an alternative to this reductionist assumption. This alternative is open to the possibility that the ultimate foundation of our entire differentiated and multilayered reality is simply not explicable reductively in terms of an anonymous material universe acting only in accordance with the operation of impersonal physical regularities. It is an alternative that views the natural universe, including human beings, as comprising a hierarchy of levels of reality, some of which emerge as irreducibly new levels of being and activity when an appropriate level of structural physical change is attained. Thus human beings can emerge or come to exist as a completely new and irreducible "whole" when a particular stage of material development or evolution is attained.

The actualization and exercise of human nature accomplishes a radically new level of reality irreducible to its material medium. Human nature is inexplicable in terms of the various sciences that explore this material medium so effectively and is best described as a manifestation of emergent reality. This concept of emergence, suggesting an alternative approach to the materialist reductionist assumption, leaves open, without assuming it, the possibility that the ultimate foundation of the multilayered universe is the benevolent creative decision of a God who is love.

The consideration of various aspects of emergence, particularly of the emergent character of human life, provides us with a context for a discussion of human love as the most remarkable expression of human emergence. It is this discussion of human love as an emergent phenomenon that I wish to devote particular attention to in the next chapter.

Ten

THE EMERGENCE OF
HUMAN LOVE

For millennia, love has attracted, and continues to attract, the passionate interest of philosophy, religion, the arts, and indeed almost every individual person. Its influence and significance are affirmed across a wide spectrum of experience and engagement. While knowing is specifically an activity of the intellect, loving is experienced as also (and chiefly) an activity of the will involving desire and engagement. Loving is not just an interiorized intellectual grasp of an object of knowledge: it is more of a voluntary intentional orientation and conscious reaching out towards and engagement with an object that we perceive, rightly or mistakenly, to be good or of value.

We use the term "love" in many different senses. We speak of loving a good wine, a beautiful landscape, a painting, a piece of music, a great novel. We love honorable deeds and just institutions. We love our countries, our pets, and even our technological devices. In specifically interpersonal terms, we love our spouse, our family, and our friends. Religious believers desire to love their God, and they are constantly exhorted by their traditions to love their neighbors and even their enemies.

The ancient Greeks had several terms to describe different

kinds of interpersonal love. These included terms such as *agape*, *eros*, and *philia*. *Agape* generally meant spiritual unselfish love of another. *Eros*, by contrast, broadly signified egocentric self-interested sensual desire for another—basically the love of another as a source of fulfillment of one's own perceived need. *Philia* signified the calmer affectionate loving relationship of friendship. These various understandings of love were not considered mutually exclusive.

As we shall consider in more detail in the following chapter, love is also the central inspiration of the Christian religion, although it is so often betrayed by those who claim to be Christians. Christianity tells us that love is the great Christian commandment and even that God himself *is* love. In elaborating on this Christian message of the primacy of love, theologians have availed themselves of the terminology of the Greek philosophers in describing love but have interpreted it in the light of Christian revelation. *Eros* is traditionally understood, often rather negatively, as signifying sensual, self-interested, exclusively this-worldly love. *Agape* is taken as primarily signifying a divinely enabled unselfish love of God.[1]

The concept of love and the concept of good are also intimately associated. We speak of the good as that which we love or desire, and we speak of love as a conscious attraction towards that which we perceive to be good or of value. *"Bonum est quod Omnia Appetunt"*—"The Good is What Everyone Desires."

However, these initial simple associations of the concepts of love and good need to be qualified. Not everything that we represent to ourselves as a good to be pursued is truly lovable. As I have mentioned, we can self-indulgently or deceptively represent as good what are in effect objectively evil deeds. Nor does everything

---

1. A perceptive and concise reconciliation of the two concepts from a Christian perspective is provided in Pope Benedict XVI's encyclical *Deus Caritas Est*.

that we love or desire thereby rank as genuinely good, however much we may seek to portray it as so.

Nevertheless, the exercise of a distinctively human capacity to love, especially when directed towards what is objectively lovable, is certainly a preeminent instance of human emergence. It is the realization of irreducible novelty and the enablement of a unique form of causality. This is true especially of interpersonal love. I want to reflect upon this remarkable relationship in which a person begins to love and grows in love with another person.

In concentrating attention upon the loving relationship that can obtain between two people, I do not wish to undervalue the remarkable altruistic love that a person can have for a wide, even all-inclusive, range of other people. We are all aware of and appreciate the witness of the astonishing philanthropic and caring love for fellow human beings expressed by heroes and heroines who belong to various religious denominations or to none. This topic is of great interest and is certainly deserving of specific attention. That my discussion here is confined primarily to a consideration of the loving relationship between two people is in no way intended to minimize the significance and great value of the broader relationship of altruistic philanthropic love, which is here referred to only incidentally and remains a topic for future, separate consideration.

Likewise, I discuss only incidentally the non-erotic love between friends, which the ancient Greeks referred to as *philia*. Love envisaged thus as friendship denotes an affectionate and caring relationship with specific other persons whom we regard as equals and companions to be valued, cared for, and cherished. This loving relationship of companionable and caring friendship has a wider range of application than the expressions of love that we designate as *eros* or *agape*, which are characteristically directed towards a particular person. Such a love of a particular person is my principal consideration here.

When we speak of such love directed towards a particular person, we must remember that, like all human activity, such love is inextricably rooted, in an anticipatory way, in a context of organic material life from which it certainly emerges but is never altogether distanced. Human love as concretely experienced in our unfolding life is rooted in our animal nature. It is important to bear this in mind for it helps us to understand the all-too-frequent shortcomings of such love and to avoid a dualist temptation to view it as an exclusively spiritual activity.

Evidence of this anticipatory biological context of human love is provided by the instinctual, emotional, and adaptive partnering behavior manifested at the level of pre-human animal life. There is ample evidence at this pre-human level of animal life of anticipatory similarities to constitutive features of loving human partnerships. (Even if swans, traditionally represented as paragons of romantic fidelity, have been shown to be unexpectedly inconstant lovers, one can at least still cite the less appealing examples of black vultures and owl monkeys as precedents of monogamous fidelity!) The various ways in which animals associate intimately, whether monogamously or otherwise, can be seen as pre-human anticipations of our experience of the many culturally diverse variations on the theme of interpersonal human love. Such comparisons constitute valuable empirical data for scientists such as sociobiologists, evolutionary theorists, developmental psychologists, and cultural anthropologists.

When applied to the human context, their research, however valuable and informative, often adopts the reductionist assumption characteristic of much contemporary science that I considered in a previous chapter. This assumption tends to seek a reductive explanation of human expressions of desires, instincts, and emotions (such as attractions, affections, and love) in terms of their origin or production from pre-human animal causes. For example, loving human responses can be viewed and analyzed as simply useful evolutionary products enabling better adaptation to a hazardous environment.

Yet do we need to read these signs of nature thus? Although my perspective recognizes the inherent subsistence of human love in a medium of material organic animal life, I would contend that such love is not confined to the physical limitations of this medium. Human love has the capacity to be emergent relative to its physical context. It can assume, at various levels of its exercise, forms of life that exceed the capacities of simply animal life. Let me indicate how this is so.

Inherent in my love of a particular person, as distinct from my altruistic disposition to humanity in general or my companionable interest in my circle of friends, is a conscious rational recognition of a particular enhancing value that she personally possesses and with which I personally wish to be intimately associated. In this context, even my initial awareness of the physical attractiveness of a particular other person intentionally envisages or recognizes a desirable value that is good for me personally to pursue and cultivate. More is involved here than my natural instinctual appreciation of the physical beauty of various individual people who I may encounter casually but towards whom I do not experience a particular personal loving attraction. From its earliest phase, the nascent love of a particular person involves a rational awareness of something of value for me, something personally desirable, enhancing, and worthy of pursuit.

This awareness of value, even in the early pursuit of love, does not automatically qualify such love as a remarkable moral achievement. The ambiguous character of love, particularly in its initial stages, usually involves a great deal of self-interest and even selfishness. I desire the value that the loved one embodies—not so much in appreciation of her intrinsic excellence but rather for my own enjoyment, satisfaction, and fulfillment. There is a significant difference between, on the one hand, deeming a person valuable and lovable because I find her desirable as representing a good for me and, on the other hand, finding her desirable because I recognize and cherish her intrinsic worth and value and love her as the subject of whom they are an expression.

An activity is not constituted as morally or objectively valuable just because it engages my loving, desiring, or wanting. The characteristics that inspire and motivate my moral recognition and appreciation of the intrinsic worth and value of my beloved, as opposed to her physical attractiveness, are disclosed by cultivated intellectual intuition and rational reflection. They are not produced by my instinctual desires or wants, although those instinctual desires can prompt an attention that my emergent and refined human motivation can discover. The value that she reveals is recognized as not simply relative to my instinctual desires.

Although even the early phase of a loving relationship is not merely instinctual and is already influenced by our human condition as rational beings capable of recognizing intrinsic value, it is a phase in which, generally speaking, one is enchanted by the way the loved one corresponds to and fulfills one's own longings, aspirations, and desires. The focus is primarily on how good she seems to be *for me*. This, of course, is an amiable and even admirable discovery but is not yet a major moral achievement. It is perhaps a pre-condition and an ongoing pre-requirement of subsequent moral progress in the art of loving.

There is no inevitable course to a loving relationship between two people. It may never get beyond an initial stage of mutual physical attraction or even, unfortunately, of only a one-sided unrequited physical attraction. It may progress into a harmonious and convenient stable relationship of mutual satisfaction, fulfillment, enjoyment, interest, support, and affection. It may flower into a wider and happy family context. However, it is liable, unless cultivated, to become simply a convenient or comfortable way of life. Unhappily it may even—and frequently does—founder and disintegrate, especially in a society marked by impermanence and change.

The term *eros*, as distinct from *agape* (which I will consider presently), may be used broadly to characterize this initial stage of a harmonious, mutually fulfilling, loving relationship between two people. Such a relationship will, of course, involve many subtle nuances and levels of significance, companionship, and generosity, and will never be precisely the same for any two couples. However, broadly speaking, this relationship is one in which the two people involved find personal satisfaction and fulfillment within the relationship. It includes a loving that is a being in love *with* another. For the two persons involved, the relationship is valued as revealing and satisfying very effectively their mutual deep-seated personal needs and desires in various ways. It is more intimate than, though not alien to, the calmer and more dispassionate loving relationship of friendship, *philia*. Hence, when this mutual fulfillment of deep-seated personal hopes, desires, and aspirations falters, the relationship, as a loving relationship, begins to fail. The two may part ways, each one's loyalty not to each other but to self.

This conventional "erotic" form of a loving relationship, aimed at the mutual fulfillment of a specific couple and involving their conscious and ongoing exercise of rational choices and commitments with this objective in view, can flourish as a life of considerable moral value. It can involve the persevering exercise of many virtues such as patience, understanding, sympathy, forgiveness, encouragement, appreciation, and gratitude. It is no mean compliment to congratulate a couple on living admirable lives characterized by a loving erotic relationship. This way of life is clearly emergent from, and quite irreducible to, the material organic context in which it subsists and from which it emerges, through rational judgment and decisions, to create its own personal version of a specifically human, erotic, loving relationship. It is not intelligible simply in terms of physical causation or as only an evolutionary product favoring reproductive fitness to which objective moral considerations are quite irrelevant.

Although to live a life of mutually fulfilling erotic love is a considerable moral achievement, it is not the only or most perfect form of human love. Erotic love can self-transcend or become transformed into a more perfect form of human love—namely, the loving relationship of *agape*, which I will consider briefly in the next chapter.

Eleven

LOVE AS AGAPE

There is a broad and venerable distinction between human love considered as *eros* and human love considered as *agape*. This distinction is between love extended to the beloved as a valued source of one's own emotional and personal enrichment and love expressed as unselfish benevolent recognition and cherishing of the intrinsic goodness and beauty of the beloved. Since the Christian era, love in its fullest and deepest sense has tended to be identified simply with *agape* and contrasted with (rather than distinguished from) erotic human love.

However, the distinction is not clear-cut.[1] With some Greek writers, such as Plato, *eros* has a deeper significance than sensual fulfillment. Plato does not refer to *agape* as a distinct kind of love. In the *Symposium* Plato develops his account of *eros*. He tells us that love is always oriented towards beauty. Its initial phase of sensual love of beautiful bodies is only the commencement of an arduous intellectual itinerary. But even this initial moment of sensuous love of physical beauty is already a primitive exercise of reason. Love of the beautiful is founded upon the emergent nature of man as a rational animal rather than a simply instinctive one. As William Stace

1. See Pope Benedict, *Deus Caritas Est*, Encyclical Letter (December 25, 2005), 2–8.

143

notes, other animals manifest no feeling for the beautiful because they are not rational.[2]

Plato's intellectual quest for beauty ascends from sensuous love through various higher forms of love of beauty and hopefully culminates in an intellectually fulfilling access to and comprehension of the idea of beauty itself:

> Begin from the beauties of earth and mount upwards for the sake of that other beauty, using these as steps only, and from one going on to two, and from two to all fair forms, and from fair forms to fair practices, and from fair practices to fair notions, until from fair notions he arrives at the notion of absolute beauty, and at last knows what the essence of beauty is.[3]

In this Platonic view of *eros*, interpersonal love is seen as, at best, a preliminary phase in the itinerary of love. The ultimate aim of this itinerary is intellectual knowledge, not of a person but of an objective idea, albeit a sublime one. Love attains its proper object in the intellectual comprehension of the idea of beauty itself. Reciprocal love between particular persons is a very elementary and potentially distracting form of love.

In the Christian era, from the time of the New Testament writers, *agape* rather than *eros* was used to characterize the most fundamental kind of true love. *Eros*, understood primarily as sensuous mutually fulfilling love between persons, was seen as inferior to the selfless love of *agape* advocated by Christian teaching. Let us consider further this distinction and the emphasis on the greater significance of love considered as *agape*.

2. W. T. Stace, *A Critical History of Greek Philosophy* (London: Macmillan, 1967), 204–6.

3. Plato, *Symposium*, in *The Dialogues of Plato*, trans. Benjamin Jowett (New York: Random House, 1937), 1:335.

Eros is basically characterized as a form of love of another who is valued primarily as motivating and fulfilling a personal need or desire. As such, it is an activity whose primary goal is not the recognition of the inherent value of the loved one but rather the fulfillment of an existential need of the lover that the loved one can motivate and provide.

However, this love, although intrinsically self-regarding, need not be mutually exclusive with the unselfish love of *agape*. In fact, it seems reasonable to maintain that the love one professes for another person is a combination of *eros* and *agape*, a combination of a self-centered fulfillment of desire and an unselfish well-wishing and promotion of the absolute and intrinsic value of the loved one. Perhaps, too, the development of *agape* for the beloved can be described as a progression by means of which the erotic self-regarding dimension, without ever disappearing, is creatively transformed into a relationship of unselfish concern for the well-being and flourishing of the beloved partner. This love, although existing in a medium of personal desire, has emerged into a higher form of regard for the beloved. The loved one is no longer viewed primarily as providing a wonderful fulfillment of the lover's deepest desires but as a being of autonomous worth and value to be cared for and greatly cherished. Such love becomes a loving relationship that includes, but also exceeds, both personal desire and intimate friendship—a relationship in which the loved one is loved primarily for what she herself is rather than for how she fulfills the lover's needs and aspirations. This loving affirmation of the loved one's intrinsic goodness and beauty of being is experienced particularly but not exclusively by her partner—in my own case through the intrinsic beauty and goodness of my beloved wife Frankie. Those who came in contact with her through friendship, or even only socially, intuitively recognized and loved her manifest quality of intrinsic goodness. At least so I have often been told by people who encountered my beloved in various circumstances.

However, it is the person who is intimately associated with the loved one as her partner and lover who can come to a particularly intense and personal recognition of her intrinsic self-possessed goodness. This recognition is not automatic, inevitable, or perhaps even customary and fully explicit. Where such emergent predominance of unselfish, loving, and benevolent regard for the loved one actually obtains, it typically does so not as a sudden conscious change of emotional gear but rather as a gradual and progressive transformation of moral outlook and orientation. Such recognition comes about as an appropriate response to a deepening and pre-reflective, but rational, lived appreciation of the intrinsic goodness, truth, and beauty of the loved one. It is the objective ontological excellence of the beloved, rather than the lover's own perceived desires or needs, that motivates and inspires the lover's unselfish other-regarding love of her.

The extent and nature of this morally developed love of one's beloved is often neither fully and reflectively apprehended nor consciously and explicitly affirmed. It may feature simply as a genuine but largely implicit and pre-reflectively experienced aspect of an inclusive habitual appreciation of and benevolent regard for one's beloved. It may only be expressed on special occasions, like a birthday or an anniversary. It may require something out of the ordinary course of events, such as a mishap or a sudden illness, to bring sharply to attention how much one's love of the beloved has evolved. One may discover, perhaps to one's surprise, that one's love of her has evolved or emerged from being primarily a form of self-regarding appreciation of her as fulfilling all one's desires. It

has become an affirmation and celebration of the intrinsic goodness and beauty of her very being, and a selfless solicitude for the
well-being of this beautiful but vulnerable reality.

Paradoxically, the nature and extent of this *agape* or unselfish
love of one's beloved is often brought to its keenest explicit awareness and affirmation only upon her death. It is as though, in her
physical absence, her reality as fulfilling my needs and desires is
less absorbing and my attention can focus more centrally on the
intrinsic goodness and beauty of her being, a goodness and beauty now sorrowfully experienced as the presence of an absence.
Included in this attention to her intrinsic goodness is a deeper
awareness of the generous and unselfish love that she devoted to
me while she was physically alive—and the hope that somehow it
still obtains.

Even after the beloved's death, this love of her inherent goodness and beauty is a love oriented to this goodness and beauty as
somehow an enduring reality and not just a memory. It seems to
challenge the presumption that there is nothing more to her than
the wonderful and desirable, but intrinsically contingent, complex
of physical atoms in which she subsisted when physically alive. She
is loved as the indestructible value she is in herself and not just as
she was for me—although her love for me is appreciated as a significant and hopefully abiding characteristic of her intrinsic goodness.

Grieving for the loss of one's beloved, particularly when one experiences a sharpened appreciation of her intrinsic goodness, is an
entirely natural and reasonable reaction. Nevertheless, even this
unselfish love towards a loved one who is no longer physically alive
can at times be deflected into a form of self-regarding consolation.
It can deteriorate into self-indulgent absorption in one's grief
wherein the goodness of the absent lover is recognized not just for

what it is in itself but as something whose loss is transfigured into a preoccupying source of tearful self-pity—almost a consoling endurance of one's profound sense of loss.

However, this temptation to transform recognition of the goodness of one's absent beloved into a form of sorrowful emotional consolation does not have to obtain or prevail. One can explicitly focus one's attention in an *agapeistic* loving relationship with the absent loved one—a loving relationship that is not self-regarding but directly recognizes, celebrates, and is solicitous for the inherent self-possessed beauty and goodness of her being. Her existence as characterized by this intrinsic beauty and goodness is affirmed and loved as an enduring value and reality and not merely as a postmortem memory or an illusion.

This loving affirmation somehow pierces the veil of contingent physical appearances and gives joyful access to an abiding excellence. It is an attentive, hopeful, loving delight in an independently possessed truth, goodness, and beauty. It is love in the "present tense" as of an actually existing person. One cannot love a cherished pet animal that has died or a much-appreciated painting that has been destroyed in this present-tense way. At most. one might reflect sadly how, in a way, one previously appreciated or "loved" them. This is love in the "past tense," utterly different from the attentively exercised actual love of one's beloved as still existing after her physical demise. One affirms "I love you," not just "I loved you." If this attentive love indeed attains a genuinely enduring reality—and not simply a cherished memory, a contingent historical trace, or an utter illusion—significant questions arise concerning how this can be so.

In the following chapter I will discuss further this love of a beloved as existing and alive beyond her physical death and will try to achieve some comprehension of what it involves. This discussion will lead on in subsequent chapters to the second main theme of this reflection: the love of God and its relationship to the love of one's beloved, which I claim can continue to exist (even after her death) as *agapeistic* love of her abiding intrinsic goodness. For me personally, it will be an exploration of how my love of God relates to and possibly vindicates my ongoing love of the abiding intrinsic goodness of my beautiful wife Frankie as a living reality rather than just a cherished memory.

Twelve

IMPLICATIONS OF LOVE

If I am not deluded in loving my beautiful Frankie as existing after her death, I find therein striking evidence of a remarkable instance of emergence. Clearly her new mode of existence and activity, whatever form they have, are neither deducible from nor reducible to the physical components of her bodily remains, even though they may have some relationship to them as to that in which she previously subsisted and from which she has decisively emerged. She is loved now as existing in a new manner, one that acclaims the continuing reality of the goodness and lovableness characteristic of her being. This goodness and lovableness are affirmed as coexistent with the personal, generous, and unselfish loving consciousness that was so manifest in her bodily existence. She is affirmed as the same conscious, beautiful, and loving person of whose embodied existence I previously had direct physical experience but who is now lovingly acclaimed as existing in a nonbodily manner.

Iris Murdoch, the novelist and philosopher, expressed a similar intuition in a less personal context in her fine essay *The Sovereignty of Good*. She remarks:

It will be said that it is a long step from the idea of realism to the idea of transcendence. I think, however, that these two ideas are related, and one can see their relation particularly in the case of our apprehension of beauty. The link here is the concept of indestructibility or incorruptibility. What is truly beautiful is "inaccessible" and cannot be possessed or destroyed. The statue is broken, the flower fades, the experience ceases, but something has not suffered from decay and mortality.[1]

The loving proclamation of the abiding existence of one's beloved is affirmed in a way that differs from whatever objective metaphysical arguments one may be able to adduce in its favor. Such arguments, however plausible, are unlikely to be entirely compelling or existentially effective. For example, we may conclude philosophically from the more than physical nature of a person's rational and voluntary capacities that, as the subjective source of these capacities, she survives the disintegration of her body. We can surmise that she somehow continues to exercise these capacities in a nonmaterial context. However, the degree of conviction afforded by such detached metaphysical speculation is very different from the degree of conviction of her abiding existence disclosed with one's unselfish love of her.

The loving affirmation of the abiding existence of my beloved even after death gives itself to my consciousness, not as an impersonally registered objective truth but as a self-involving and profoundly affecting assurance. It is as though, through the medium of love (hers? mine? both?), the abiding reality of my inherently good and lovable life partner is given, however tenuously, to my hopeful longing and conscious desire in an intimate and personal manner. One attains an intimation, animated by love, of the unperceived reality of one's absent beloved. It is an intimation imbued with the reasonable hope that what is valuable, beautiful, and good, rather than what is contingent and corruptible, is what ultimately real-

1. Iris Murdoch, *The Sovereignty of Good* (London: Routledge and Kegan Paul, 1970), 59.

ly obtains. This loving and reasonable hope culminates in a joyful self-involving affirmative belief.

I am not referring here to the traditional theological virtues of faith, hope and charity, although I may be describing a secular anticipation of them. I am trying to describe a kind of rational belief in the assured reality of my beautiful wife, a reality that is given to me not through philosophizing abstractly about her or simply remembering her but in and through my non-self-regarding love of and solicitude for her inherent goodness and beauty of spirit as an enduring reality. This love gives a manner of access to my beloved that is not available to detached impersonal inquiry. It is as though she "tunes in" personally to my love of her in a manner that is not accessible to impersonal description. She discloses herself to my awareness as a gift rather than as an argued conclusion.

It is not easy to elucidate this knowledge of one's beloved disclosed through loving attention rather than through metaphysical argument. However, recourse to a couple of analogies may help. One of these adverts to the nature of our aesthetic experiences. The other has recourse to the French philosopher Jean-Luc Marion's illuminating concept of a "saturated phenomenon," which we discussed in the chapter on theism.

Consider an experience of aesthetic delight—for example, the experience of a physically beautiful person, a beautiful landscape, or a beautiful sculpture. It is susceptible to at least two very different kinds of description involving two different modes of discourse. One of these can be called intentional—subject-related or phenomenological discourse. The other is the detached objective discourse of experimental science. We can discuss an aesthetic experience phenomenologically by means of a detailed description of the essential structure of how the beautiful object appears to and impacts us, as it resonates with but also transforms our prior experience and occasions our delighted awareness of it. Or we can describe our aesthetic experience scientifically in terms of the physical, physiological, and neurological processes that render it possible. Each discourse has its own kind of validity, but the phenomenological is more adequate to our experience of beauty as it gives itself to our consciousness. Likewise the consciousness of my beloved's abiding reality, which loving attention to the intrinsic goodness of one's beloved intimates, is usually more personally relevant and significant than an objective metaphysical account of its possibility. (Needless to say, this superiority of the phenomenological over the scientific or metaphysical does not always obtain. For example, when we experience a sharp pain in our chest, we wisely resort to a physician and not to a phenomenologist such as Jean-Luc Marion for elucidation!)

In chapter 3 we saw how Marion develops an account of what he calls the "saturated phenomenon." For him, every phenomenon that shows itself in experience does so only to the extent that it gives itself first. This has the noteworthy implication that the subject of experience is not seen as wholly or primarily determining the conditions of whatever can be given in experience.

For the most part, the intentional capacity and activity of the knowing subject undoubtedly enables, constitutes, or structures the phenomena that are given in experience. When we experience a piece of colored cloth attached to a pole, we perceive or construe it as a national flag. The humanly experienced world that we constructively navigate is very different to that experienced by a rabbit or a mouse.

However, according to Marion, some phenomena, as they give themselves in experience, are intuited as exceeding, overflowing, and utterly saturating the subject's capacity to envisage, conceptualize, or constitute the manner in which they give themselves. The subject does not determine the manner of the phenomena's appearance. Rather, the phenomena themselves, as saturated, transform and enable the subject to experience them. They are phenomena manifesting themselves as unique and unanticipated. They overwhelm and transform our conscious subjectivity rather than being circumscribed or constituted by it. In relation to these phenomena, the role of our subjectivity is that of a passive recipient. By virtue of its sheer susceptible passivity, our subjectivity enables these phenomena to manifest themselves in a manner such that it finds itself *subject to*, not *the subject of*, such saturated phenomena.

Marion applies his account of saturated phenomena to the area of religious experience and affirms the possibility of a phenomenologically given but non-conceptualizable intuition of God as incomprehensible—such as one finds, although not exclusively, in accounts of overwhelming mystical experience. For a more secular instance of a saturated phenomenon, he cites the example of a painter who makes visible a phenomenon by being the first who, through her success in creatively "resisting" a given profound experience, enables it to manifest itself for the first time in a disclosing artistic phenomenon accessible to all.[2] To elucidate this conception of a saturated phenomenon as a creatively resisted experience, Marion draws attention to the suggestive image of electrical resistance wherein the restriction of the free movement of electrons in a cable transforms their invisible movement into phenomenalized light and heat.[3]

2. Jean-Luc Marion, "The Event, the Phenomenon and the Revealed," in *Transcendence in Philosophy and Religion*, ed. James E. Faulconer (Bloomington: Indiana University Press, 2003), 103.

3. Ibid., 103.

As I indicated, I have difficulty with the suggestion that we can experience divine transcendence phenomenologically, even as a saturated phenomenon. However, perhaps the loving affirmation of the abiding existence of one's beloved can be helpfully viewed as a saturated phenomenon. Her enduring reality is primarily affirmed not as a metaphysically established conclusion but as a gift, enabled by my loving, receptive, and attentive disposition in her regard. She is intuited not as an accurately remembered object of my ordinary intending consciousness but as the enigmatic presence of one who is absent, a person who is enabled to manifest herself as an absent reality to my unselfish, solicitous, loving attention. My receptive, un-self-regarding, loving attention attains her, not as an object of ordinary perception but as an enigmatic disclosure. It is by my receptive, patient, and solicitous attention to her intrinsic goodness, loved for itself, that her presence as absent reality is enabled to give and manifest itself. It manifests itself unpredictably, enigmatically, and overwhelmingly as a saturated phenomenon utterly beyond my ability to constitute, determine, or manipulate it. She is manifest as a gift, a mysterious given or invocation, bestowed uniquely and occasionally to my loving attention in a way that exceeds any concept I can fashion of her.

These indications about the personal character of aesthetic experience and the compelling unconstituted character of saturated phenomena help to elucidate the emergent quality both of the continued existence after death of my beloved Frankie and of my subjective knowledge of it, made accessible through my loving, receptive, and hopeful attention to her intrinsic goodness and beauty of spirit. Her continued existence, affirmed as obtaining and acting in a manner neither deducible from nor reducible to the physical remains from which it has emerged, resembles the way in which a saturated phenomenon gives itself as neither deducible from nor reducible to the routine constitutive intentional activity through which we fashion and organize our direct experiences. In both instances, we have a reality given in a manner that is inexplicable in terms of its temporal or physical antecedents. Likewise, one's subjective or personal knowledge of this continued existence resembles the personal character of an aesthetic experience of a beautiful object, which differs from the objective or impersonal knowledge of it provided through scientific description of the physical and neurological processes involved.

It is important, however, to acknowledge that the awareness of the abiding existence of one's beloved is an awareness of her presence as absence. It is not a perceptual experience of her presence. Such was my awareness of her incarnate presence and, hopefully, will also be my awareness when we meet again after my physical death. The most one can affirm now is an experiential awareness of an absence that is not simply a negation or denial of existence. It is not merely a sad recognition of the end of a personal history. It is rather, and astonishingly, awareness, accessible through love, hope, and faith, of the presence as absence of the abiding reality of one's beloved.

One may even speak of the newly *emergent* reality of my beloved enabling my loving attention to and affirmation of her presence as absent abiding reality—a reality that is distinct from my previous perceptual experience or loving memory of her physical existence. To make such a claim is not to contradict the remark above that it is *my* loving attention to her goodness that enables the knowledge of her continued existence after death. Consider, for example, Marion's account of how a saturated phenomenon, such as the experience of a given reality as beautiful, surpasses the intentional capacities of ordinary human subjectivity and transforms this subjectivity by enabling it to be the receptive vehicle of the manifestation of the saturated phenomenon. Similarly, my beloved's emergent reality after death enables my love of her intrinsic goodness to reach a new and deeper level of experience.

One might say that here my agapeistic love, my love of my beloved simply for herself and not primarily as corresponding to my own needs or desires, achieves a status that is emergent even relative to the form in which it previously tended to find expression when she was still incarnate in the world of ordinary perception. This was a way of loving her, characteristically in a somewhat unreflected-upon or taken-for-granted manner, involving an admixture of self-regarding erotic desire and selfless benevolent love of her intrinsic goodness. My agapeistic love of her now involves loving her in a different manner as possessing a very different way of being. This more sustained transformation of my love from selfishness to unselfishness enables a certain transcendence of self-indulgent imagining to an awareness of her as participating in the ultimate real triumph of goodness over corruptibility and contingency.

If accepted as genuine and not merely an illusion or an instance of wish fulfillment, this love of my beloved Frankie, giving phenomenological access to her different mode of being as beyond my capacity to conceive or constitute, invokes further reflection about the objective conditions of its possibility. It is not enough to simply affirm the genuineness of the given phenomena that disclose this personal experience of loving my beautiful wife as existing after her death. I should also seek to determine, and if possible confirm, the objective or theoretical truth conditions that must obtain if this affirmation is to describe a genuine reality and be impervious to the charge that it is merely an illusion. Further philosophical and theological reflection is required for this consideration of the conditions that would have to obtain in order to confirm the truth of the self-involving assertion that I reliably love my beautiful wife Frankie as enjoying a continued and loving personal existence beyond her physical death. Such reflection leads me on to a discussion of the love of God, which is the second major theme of my personal itinerary or inquiry into ultimate meaning and value.

Thirteen

LOVE AND FAITH

The relationship between belief in the abiding reality of someone you dearly love, even after her physical death, and belief in a loving God presents itself as an important theme—especially for Christian faith. As St. Paul insists, if Christ is not alive, risen as promised to glorious life after a harrowing death, our Christian faith is discredited.[1] It would thereby be shown to be a profound delusion. Equally significant for me is my conviction that if my beloved Frankie does not exist and continue to live, to know, and to love after her physical death, then the Christian affirmation of a saving risen Christ is also a profound delusion. For a Christian like me, whose cherished wife has died, belief in Christ as truly God (who has disproved the alleged finality and ultimacy of death) and belief in her abiding existence are intrinsically related. Deny the risen Christ, and the affirmation of the abiding existence of one's beloved can appear to be a very fallible assertion, perhaps a futile desire or a grief-induced exercise in wish fulfillment. Deny the continued existence after death of one's beloved, and the affirmation of the existence of the risen Christ as truly a saving God, who has assured the beloved's continued existence, would be an empty claim.

1. 1 Cor 15:14 (this and all subsequent biblical translations come from the Jerusalem Bible).

The stakes involved in this relationship could not be higher. Unless each term of the relationship signifies an abiding real existence, neither is entirely credible. Nevertheless, what is affirmed in the alleged relationship is more than I can know with certitude through the exercise of my natural reason alone. What this belief involves is more than any natural belief involves—for example, my belief that Ireland is an island, the truth of which I could readily confirm for myself.

Undoubtedly the exercise of natural reason can offer some support both for belief in the possible survival of one's beloved and for belief in the existence of an infinitely perfect God. However, such reasoning falls far short of this disclosure, even if it provides a rational infra-structure that is compatible with and supportive of what is disclosed in Christian revelation to the faith of the believer. A believer's faith in Christian revelation is of a different order than his belief in something that he currently believes on the basis of authority but that later, should he wish, he could find out for himself by an appropriate use of his natural powers of observation and reason. Most of our cognitive claims are natural beliefs of this kind. The belief characteristic of Christian faith is different, and this difference is indicated by terming it a divinely enabled or graced belief.

Traditionally the Christian's act of faith is understood to involve three main components: intellectual comprehension, commitment of the will, and an enabling divine gift of grace. The act of faith is voluntary but not arbitrary. It involves rational comprehension and intellectual conviction. However, since it is a commitment to the truth of a divine revelation that is beyond the range of natural human reason, its attainment implies the enabling support of divine help or grace. Although this enabling divine grace is an indispensable component of the "supernatural" virtue of faith, it does not dispense with the contributions of the other two components. The belief in the revealed truth professed by the believer, even though beyond the range of natural reason, is affirmed as an intellectually justifiable, reliably motivated, and freely exercised commitment to God's revelation accepted as such.

The intellectual justification of the Christian faith can involve different features and stages. For example, it can involve various philosophical affirmations concerning the existence and nature of God, sometimes referred to as the *preambulae fidei* or the rational presuppositions of faith. Traditionally the philosophical consideration of these rational presuppositions is called natural theology. It includes various metaphysical proofs for the existence of God as creator of the world and the derivation of various true statements about the characteristics of God as thus envisaged. As we considered earlier, there are also various phenomenological and linguistic philosophical approaches to the affirmation of God.

Further, the intellectual justification of faith involves showing that the propositions affirmed by faith, although not provable by natural reason, are at least not contradictory to natural reason and are comprehensible independently of faith—that is, their meaning is equally accessible to both believers and nonbelievers (given proper study or exposure). The intellectual justification of faith also involves attending to the historical evidence of God's revelation provided by the testimony and teaching of people of great holiness, integrity, and prophetic witness—a revelation most perfectly manifested and exemplified in the life, death, and resurrection of Jesus.

There are also the intimate interior religious experiences of each individual, which illuminate and sustain each individual's personal conviction that his or her faith embodies a genuine communion with God. The grace-enabled loving adhesion of the will to what is disclosed in divine revelation is appreciated as a reasonable commitment, not just an arbitrary decision.

The fruitful interaction of faith's three components—understanding, willing commitment, and divine grace—provides assurance that faith in the God of Christian revelation is neither naïve credulity, nor an arbitrary choice, nor a mere hypothesis. Rather, faith is an intellectually defensible and rationally motivated commitment to an objective ultimate reality, affirmed as compatible with but transcending what is accessible through the intrinsic resources of natural reason alone.

Close attention to the intellectual component in a discussion of the justification of faith is undoubtedly important. I have considered aspects of this in earlier chapters. However, here I propose to focus attention on the other main human component in the act of faith—namely, the involvement of the will. For it is through such attentive reflection that the theme of the love of God can be addressed in a particularly pertinent and revealing manner.

Love is never simply an instance of detached speculative observation. It is always a form of voluntary engagement, a way of desiring, pursuing, and promoting what an individual perceives to be good. It is a conscious affirmative orientation of the will towards whatever or whomever is perceived to be good, with a view to acclaiming this goodness and desiring somehow to participate in or be associated with it. Although one can be said to love various material goods in a rather minimal sense, love in its truest form is a conscious attraction to and affirmation of a *personal* goodness that one has encountered or envisages. This is certainly true of genuine love of one's beloved wife or husband. It is also and particularly true of genuine love of God.

When we speak of "the love of God," we can mean either our love of him or his love of us. In the next chapter I will reflect upon the first aspect—namely, our love of him and how it might be related to our love of a greatly beloved person (for me personally my love of my beautiful wife). In the following chapter I will reflect upon his love of us and its specific bearing upon our belief in the abiding existence of our loved one.

Fourteen

OUR NATURAL LOVE OF GOD

A minimal implication of my claim to love God is that I believe in his real existence as infinite goodness and perfection. I suggest that this is an implication rather than a condition of my claim to love God because I want to leave open the possibility that the claim to know that he exists is in a way attainable through the act of loving itself. This approach will involve a development of the claim of St. Augustine, which we discussed in chapter 7, that it is only through love that one has access to ultimate truth.

This, of course, is a debatable contention. It is immediately open to an accusation of wish fulfillment, as though by attempting to love God one could somehow adduce his existence. Surely, it might be reasonably objected, it is only when we already know that God exists and is infinitely lovable that we can love him.

Nevertheless, I do not wish to exclude *a priori* the possibility that some intimation of the existence of God can be attained through a loving desire for and openness to whatever is good—which, on reflection, is ultimately found to be an attraction to God himself, who exists as infinite goodness. It may transpire that through faith in divine revelation, we can come to a fuller theological realization that God, affirmed as infinite goodness, exists as the ultimate fulfillment of our phenomenologically experienced and seemingly unrestricted loving desire for what is good. St. Augustine expressed this supposition more dramatically when he wrote: "Thou hast made us for thyself O Lord and our hearts are restless until they rest in thee."

One can, of course, address the topic of the love of God simply from a detached objective philosophical perspective. As indicated in our discussion of theism, one can argue metaphysically from various features of our experience that God exists as the infinitely perfect creator of all finite realities (including ourselves). Such arguments are formulated in various proofs for the existence of God, such as the famous "Five Ways" of Thomas Aquinas, which argue that God exists as the ultimate rationale of the mutability, dependent nature, contingency, analogical diversity, and purposeful activity of the finite realities of our experience. God affirmed in this way could be recognized as deserving our religious veneration and worship. The God worshipped in such natural religious veneration could surely be revered as deserving our loving acknowledgment as the one who created us. However, this loving recognition falls very short of the Christian revelation of how we can and should love God.

Aquinas views such natural religious sentiment as pertaining more to the moral virtue of justice than to the theological virtue of charity or love. In Aquinas's account, religion is a virtuous activity of rendering to God the honor and worship that are his due. Whatever genuine element of love is involved in such natural religious sentiment is embedded in, and possibly qualified by, a circumspect sense of dependence and maybe even of precautionary deference. "The beginning of wisdom is the fear of the Lord."

Perhaps, as I suggested earlier, a reconsideration of St. Anselm's famous ontological argument for the existence of God can provide a more benign and illuminating perspective on our natural capacity to love God. This argument claims that from our idea or description of God as "a being than which none greater or better can be conceived," we can conclude directly to God as existing in reality, not just as a formulated notion in our mind. For since it is obviously greater to exist in reality than to exist as just a concept in the mind, and since God is designated as the being than which nothing greater can be conceived, he must be understood to exist in reality and not merely as a concept in our minds.

I have always considered this argument unconvincing as a strictly logical or metaphysical argument. For it assumes that we can know *a priori* that our description of God as a being than which nothing greater can be conceived is coherent and signifies something positively possible and noncontradictory.

It seems to me, however, that before we know that God indeed exists, the most we can say about our notion of him as "that than which nothing greater can be conceived" is that it is only a negatively possible notion or description—that is, we do not know whether what it seeks to represent is positively possible or positively impossible. We do not know metaphysically whether our *a priori* description of God as "that than which nothing greater can be conceived" is coherent or perhaps contradictory, like the concept of a square circle. We thus do not prove the existence of God metaphysically from our *a priori* knowledge of the positive possibility, coherence, and noncontradictory character of our description of him. On the contrary, we prove the positive possibility, coherence, and conceptual validity of our linguistic description of him by proving his existence *a posteriori* through indirect philosophical argument from features of the world we directly experience.

However, perhaps the matter can be addressed in another way that emphasizes the significance of our voluntary love of the good in facilitating an affirmation of God. Perhaps the reference to God as "that than which nothing greater can be conceived" can be reformulated more accurately as "that which is greater or better than anything which we can conceive." This signifies that God, if he exists, is beyond any reality that we might be able to represent conceptually. In Wittgensteinian terminology, what God is does not fall under our ordinary use of language—he is the mystical. This reformulation is a signaling that God is not contained within the order of finite beings whose components we are capable of representing conceptually.

If God exists, he does so as infinite reality, which is beyond the range of our conceptual representation. As Jean-Luc Marion observes, the true force of Anselm's argument is that "if we know that God is, we attain this knowledge by means of the concept that we have no concept of Him, rather than through the concept that we do."[1] God is envisaged not as a reality that we can positively comprehend or conceptually represent but rather as incomprehensible mystical reality, of which we have an intimation that if it exists, it does so in a manner beyond that of any finite reality that we might be able to adequately represent conceptually.

Moreover, as Marion points out, this paradoxical notion or intimation of divine infinity of which we can form no positively intelligible concept is signaled more appropriately, as Anselm himself appreciated, in terms of qualitative rather than quantitative greatness. It is signaled as the notion of that which is *better* than anything conceivable. That which is greatest is signaled not as the incomprehensible greatest magnitude or power but as the incomprehensible greatest goodness. Such a notion or intimation of incomprehensi-

1. Jean-Luc Marion, *Cartesian Questions: Method and Metaphysics*, trans. and ed. Jeffrey Kosky (Chicago: University of Chicago Press, 1999), 157.

ble infinite goodness, transcending any particular finite good that we might conceive, spontaneously engages our yearning and loving desire. We lovingly desire infinite goodness to really obtain or actually be the case, and to thereby confirm and vindicate the reasonable hope that being is ultimately, intrinsically, and dependably good rather than contingent and meaningless.

Admittedly, one cannot reason directly from our natural seemingly limitless desire for what is good and lovable to the real existence of God envisaged as incomprehensible infinite goodness. But one can envisage that his existence is implicit in this desire in the sense that if infinite goodness truly obtains, it would indeed and uniquely constitute the adequate fulfillment of our seemingly limitless desire for the good that no limited and contingent good that we directly experience or conceive can comprehensively satisfy. Undoubtedly this implication needs to be made explicit by further reflection and reasoning. Recall St. Thomas Aquinas's perceptive remark: "Now, man naturally desires God in so far as he naturally desires happiness, which is a certain likeness of the divine goodness. On this basis, it is not necessary that God considered in Himself be naturally known to man, but only a likeness of God. It remains, therefore, that man is to reach the knowledge of God through reasoning by way of the likeness of God found in His effects."[2]

Our seemingly unrestricted loving desire for what is good and lovable—envisaged as not completely fulfilled by any limited, contingent, and fallible goodness that we might conceptually represent—enables us to entertain at least the negative and unverified possibility of unrestricted and supremely desirable goodness. This is true despite the fact that formulating an adequate concept

---

2. Thomas Aquinas, *Summa contra Gentiles* I, ch. 3.

of such goodness is beyond our capacity. Our experiential openness, through loving desire, to this goodness beyond any comprehensible finite good can be interpreted as a reasonable hope that God envisaged thus as infinite goodness, though not conceptually apprehended or comprehended, may nevertheless indeed exist. By further reflection and reasoning, we may subsequently attain a personal existential conviction that this infinite goodness, the incomprehensible object of our love and rational hope, indeed exists as the infinite goodness of God. We can appreciate the force of Wittgenstein's aforementioned observation that "if there is a value which is of value, it must lie outside all happening and being-so."[3]

Marion argues, more directly, that in virtue of this limitless capacity of ours to love and desire, we are able to transcend our limited conceptual capacity to form humanly intelligible concepts of various kinds of finite goodness and thereby to experience some intuitive perceptible awareness of God's incomprehensible goodness. Marion claims that through the engagement of our unrestricted desire for and love of the good, we can affirm an experience of God as infinite goodness being given in an obscure or dazzling perception. This possibility is envisaged as the saturated phenomenon that we name "the idea of infinity." It is a possibility of God being given to our consciousness as the desirable supreme good, a "being given" that is not precluded by our own limited conceptual capacity to only form concepts of various kinds of finite goodness. For Marion, the profound significance of this awareness of God's givenness as supreme goodness is elucidated *theologically* in the historical Christian revelation to faith. This revelation elaborates the actuality of God as self-giving love who has incorporated us into his divine life of love.

3. Wittgenstein, *Tractatus logico-philosophicus*, 6.41.

I have indicated elsewhere some reservations about Marion's claim that an appropriate interpretation of Anselm's argument philosophically confirms that the existence of God, envisaged as incomprehensible infinite goodness, can be given intuitively to our consciousness.[4] It seems to me that we do not have any direct experience, intuitive awareness, or dazzling perception of God. For my part, I cannot claim any such awareness or perception.

It seems to me that at most what we experience by way of loving desire and reasonable hope is a finite indication or cipher of God's existence as infinite goodness. For example, our loving appreciation of a beloved person's intrinsic goodness can enable a hopeful affirmation of it as irreducible to and somehow transcending the domain of contingency and mortality in which it subsists or has subsisted. We are drawn by the consideration that such an enigmatic affirmation, deciphered by loving desire, can attain, in yearning and rational hope, an affirmation of an incomprehensible infinite goodness. Such infinite goodness would be the ultimate enabling confirmation of the initial loving affirmation of the goodness of one's beloved as transcending her incarnate contingency and physical death. This loving hopeful intimation can engender a personal existential affirmation, which may be further developed through impersonal philosophical argument or through faith in God's revelation. Similarly, one's personal profound religious experiences of the presence of God can be understood as an obscure awareness or cipher of him, a cipher that will be fully deciphered and revealed in the beatific vision.

However, I think Marion makes an important point in emphasizing the role of love and desire in achieving a personal conviction

4. Patrick Masterson, *Approaching God: Between Phenomenology and Theology* (New York: Bloomsbury, 2013), 132–35.

of the existence of God as distinct from a metaphysical proof for his existence. Marion brings clearly to our attention the important consideration that "that which is greater than anything we can conceive" is identified by Anselm not quantitatively but as "that than which there can be nothing better." Considered thus in terms of value or desirability, that which is envisaged as better than anything humanly comprehensible spontaneously engages our desire and inspires our love in a way that facilitates a personal affirmation of God. As elucidated by Marion, Anselm's specification of God's greatness as infinite goodness, rather than as merely infinite magnitude or power, discloses to our conscious loving desire for what is good an intimation of goodness beyond any concept we might form. The notion of God existing as infinite incomprehensible goodness spontaneously engages, in a unique way, our capacity to love and desire. This capacity manifests itself as a desire for a goodness that is not contingent, an unfailing goodness, and an ontologically assured goodness that necessarily exists. This desire for goodness is radically different from—and makes ultimate sense of—the various contingent and determinate kinds of finite goodness that we experience or that we might form a specific concept of.

For Marion, Anselm's significant insight involves accepting that our recognition of the actuality of God's existence cannot be disassociated from a non-humanly constructed but somehow given intimation of him as incomprehensible infinite goodness and therefore supremely lovable. Anselm appreciated that an incomprehensible infinite goodness—beyond all fallible, contingent, and finite instances of goodness that we might experience or conceive—would be the adequate ground and explanation of the existence not only of all such finite goodness but also of its own existence. We can grasp with Anselm that only of such an infinitely good and lovable reality is it inappropriate to question the self-explanatory nature of its existence.

But what, one may ask, exempts God thus envisaged as infinite inconceivable goodness (even though not comprehended as such) from requiring the sort of intelligible ground or necessary condition of his existence that we deem reasonable to seek for the existence of everything else? Why does the existence of God envisaged as infinite goodness require no account of its necessary and sufficient conditions when proposed as ultimate reality, unlike, for example, the existence of the Big Bang, which produced the primitive system of physical particles? Why is Richard Dawkins's question "Who made God?" a meaningless question? How is his existence such that, unlike anything else, it could have no further explanation? What exempts God from requiring the sort of explanatory justification of his existence that we demand of the existence of everything else?

The only, but adequate, answer to such questions is the affirmation that the existence of infinite goodness, if indeed such exists, is self-explanatory. If infinite goodness actually exists, it is futile or otiose to ask for further explanation, to demand justification, or to seek the necessary conditions that enable it to be so—in contrast with the way in which we can always so ask about any finite good and desirable state of affairs. Such a line of questioning would amount to asking why it is rationally appropriate, desirable, and self-justifyingly good that what ultimately exists is rationally appropriate, desirable, and self-justifyingly good. If infinite goodness exists, the only thing we can say by way of "explaining" such existence is that it exists because it is infinite goodness. Its existence and its goodness are identical. It is because it is infinite goodness that it exists uncaused as infinite being. It is because it is infinite being that it exists uncaused as infinite goodness and is therefore desirable and lovable. Only in existing infinite goodness is there absolute identity of what is and of what is unconditionally desirable. Only infinite goodness would be and is its own *raison d'etre*—the absolute coincidence of the ontological and the axiological, of what is and of what is desirable.

God, envisaged thus as infinite goodness, is acknowledged by Kant as "*an ideal without a flaw*, a concept which completes and crowns the whole of human knowledge."[5] Thus considered, God satisfies reason's own legitimate quest for completely sufficient explanations. Undoubtedly this affirmation does not constitute an impersonal metaphysical *a priori* proof of God's existence. However, a personal affirmation of his existence may justifiably arise from the rationality of an individual's loving desire for and hope in his existence as the infinite goodness that would be the ultimate, adequate, self-sufficient, and self-explanatory source of the meaning and value of her life. This affirmation is based on the rationality of the hope and desire that ultimately, and notwithstanding the contingency affecting our lives and the objects of our experience, reality is intrinsically and dependably good. It is an affirmation that accords with Kant's argument, outlined in chapter 4 of this book, that it is rational to affirm the existence of God as the necessary and sufficient condition of the rational coherence of our moral requirement to seek the *summum bonum*.

We may not see a necessary connection between knowing by way of metaphysical argument that God created us and being naturally disposed to love him. We may respect, fear, and worship him circumspectly as creator without necessarily appreciating that as such he is eminently worthy of our love. It is the intimation of him

5. Kant, *Critique of Pure Reason*, A641/B769.

as infinite goodness, beyond any goodness of which we can form a determinate concept, that naturally attracts us to desire and to love him. It establishes him, for us, as the God whom it is appropriate to love and not merely to worship.

Perhaps the abstract objective metaphysical approach to the existence of God as creator and the more existential self-involving phenomenological and hopeful approach that affirms the existence of God as supremely lovable require and complement each other. God may be both our creator and the ultimate personal Subject with whom we can rationally hope to somehow have a loving relationship. But how can this be and what does it involve?

Metaphysical reflections on the possibility and way of loving God are rather thin in detailed information. Philosophically we may be able to argue to the existence of God as the infinite creator of all finite beings who, since he is characterized most significantly for us humans as infinite perfection, is therefore an appropriate object of our love and desire. However, it is not at all philosophically obvious how or whether this incomprehensible lovable goodness of God can be adequately articulated or how our love of him should find expression. Perhaps the issue might be helpfully addressed initially by reflective consideration of our appreciation of the intrinsic goodness we have experienced in the actions and lives of other people.

From a natural human perspective, we might surmise philosophically that the multifaceted intrinsic goodness and lovableness of other people, which we concretely experience, provide a remote indication, trace, or cipher of the infinite goodness and lovableness of God. Thus, for example, my lived experience of the intrinsic goodness of my beloved Frankie, and my conviction that it survives unextinguished by her physical death, can serve as an indication, intimation, or cipher of the intrinsic infinite goodness of God. My love of the intrinsic goodness of my beautiful wife—not just as a memory but as an abiding personal reality, existing as emergent relative to her previous incarnate existence—can provide me with an interiorized existential intimation of God's superlative goodness as ultimate vindication of this reality and an appropriate object of my love. Her goodness as a finite cipher of his infinite goodness provides an existentially engaging phenomenological trace of this superlative goodness. I have an indirect implicit intimation of his infinite goodness as the creative, sustaining, and exemplary cause of her finite abiding goodness whose reality I have vividly experienced and continue to lovingly affirm. My love of her abiding goodness and my love of the infinite goodness of God are intimately related—as cipher and ultimate deciphering vindication. My rational hope that her intrinsic goodness transcends her experience of physical contingency would find rational justification in the existence of its necessary and sufficient condition. This would be the existence of God, envisaged as infinite goodness, who provides an ultimate and adequate justification of my conviction that my beloved's goodness, experienced as intrinsic to her nature and activity, is more ultimately real than the contingency and facticity exemplified by her physical demise.

This personal conviction might be developed more impersonally by metaphysical reflection on the necessary and sufficient condition of a finite universe characterized by both radical contingency and intrinsic personal value. Such reflection may lead to the affirmation of an infinitely good and perfect God as creator of this universe. However, its full significance only becomes apparent in the light of the Christian revelation of the ultimate nature and meaning of our loving relationship with God. In the following short chapters, I will consider God's love for us and how we are invoked to respond to it from a more theological than philosophical perspective. This invocation is disclosed to us in the Christian revelation of the nature of this divine love. This disclosure goes beyond the reach of philosophical speculation, whether theoretical or practical, and provides an astonishing transformation of our purely philosophical comprehension of our natural human condition.

Fifteen

GOD'S LOVE FOR US

In the Christian faith, the idea of love of God is revealed as having a dramatically more profound significance than is accessible through the philosophical reflection of natural reason alone. In discussing this revelation, it is helpful to begin by disclosing what it tells us about God's love for us before addressing its account of how we, in turn, are invoked to love God.

"This is the love I mean: not our love for God, but God's love for us when he sent his Son to be the sacrifice that takes our sins away."[1] And again: "God loved the world so much that he gave his only Son, so that everyone who believes in him may not be lost but may have eternal life."[2]

Undoubtedly, pre-Christian Greek and Roman thinkers had interesting observations about the appropriateness of human beings venerating and even loving their god(s). However, the idea that their god might love them, as distinct from perhaps caring for them or manipulating them, would have seemed entirely incongruous, indeed impossible. For them, love was chiefly understood as a form of desire or need—a striving or aspiration of the needy or the lower towards the higher or more perfect (seen in our previous

1. 1 Jn 4:10.
2. Jn 3:16.

177

discussion of *eros* in Plato). From such a viewpoint, it would make little sense to speak of god or gods, conceived as the most perfect dimension of the world, actually loving less perfect realities of the world such as us.

All of this changes with the Christian conception of divine love. Here, astonishingly, God is revealed not simply as provident lover of his creation (a God who might be known by our natural reason to exist as infinite goodness) but also as elevating us into a unique loving relationship. The full significance of this revolutionary idea is quite beyond the realm of philosophical discovery.

If we remain exclusively at the level of philosophical reflection, we can speak truly of God's love for us but only in a limited sense. Thus Aquinas remarks that, as infinite goodness and as cause of all that exists, God wills the good of what he has created and "since to love anything is nothing else than to will the good of that thing God loves everything that exists."[3]

If we remain at this philosophically accessible level of our relationship to God, we might consider him principally as having a providential loving interest in our wellbeing analogous to our biblically based requirement to be solicitous for the welfare of the world placed in our care. It would be difficult to envisage this loving relationship in terms of interpersonal love, which has a connotation of friendship and equality. The ontological difference between the transcendent God and the totally dependent creature is more radical and profound than the difference in level of being between a conscientious *vigneron* and his "lovingly" cultivated vineyard. An interpersonal relationship of love implies a context of equality and a capacity for reciprocal friendship. It is more a matter of "being in love with" than "having love for." Such interpersonal love between

3. Aquinas, *Summa theologiae* I, q. 20, art. 2.

creature and creator exceeds the scope of philosophical expectation or confirmation.

Because we have been enabled, through divine grace, to become more than mere creatures and thereby to participate in God's own life of love, we can speak, in a new sense, of God's love of us. As the theologian Herbert McCabe remarks, "'In Christ' we are taken up into the exchange of love between the Father and the incarnate and human Son, we are filled with the Holy Spirit, and we become part of the divine life. We call this 'grace.' By grace we ourselves share in the divine."[4]

This disclosure that we have been elevated beyond the status of mere creatures to being loved by God as participants in his divine life is an astonishing revelation. It provides a dramatic response to a significant strand of contemporary atheism that rejects, in the name of human autonomy and freedom, the understanding of human existence as just the creature of an infinite, even if provident, creator.

The revelation that we are loved by God as participants in his divine life brings the discussion of our relationship with him to an entirely different level. It is revealed as a relationship of endowed friendship and equality rather than one of servant and inferior. "I shall not call you servants any more, because a servant does not know his master's business; I call you friends, because I have made known to you everything I have learnt from my father."[5]

I think that one might describe this transformation of human nature as the most profound instance of the phenomenon of emergence, which has been a guiding theme throughout this reflection. Recall how I describe something as an emergent entity when it

4. Herbert McCabe, *God Still Matters* (London: Continuum, 2002), 7.
5. Jn 15:15.

presents itself as a unified whole manifesting properties that are neither deducible from nor reducible to the intrinsic capacities of its constituent parts or the relationships between them. As such, it is also capable of exercising a distinctive causal activity. Clearly the transformation of a human person from being simply something created by God to being a participant in God's own life, and capable of loving and being loved by him as thus participating, is a remarkable instance of the phenomenon of emergence. It indicates, as I will suggest later, a conception of emergence from which previous more "natural" examples of emergence and indeed the whole of creation can be perceptively conceived as revealing their ultimate goal or purpose.

The revelation that we are loved by God is developed into a rich theology of our incorporation into God's own life. Jesus proclaims that the ultimate truth about him is that he is loved by the Father. And, as McCabe observes, "by grace, by our receiving the Holy Spirit, by sharing in the death and life of Christ, this becomes the ultimate thing about us too. Not that we are created but that we are loved."[6] Our divinization, by grace, elevates us to participate in the life of love that is the Blessed Trinity.

Moreover, through our fidelity to this revelation, we are assured of eternal life. We are assured that what appears obscurely to us, through faith, as a reasonable and hopeful expectation in our present temporal reality will be utterly transformed to reveal itself as a wonderful directly experienced reality into which we enter joyfully, awakening from our present temporal reality as from a dream. "Now we are seeing a dim reflection in a mirror, but then we shall be seeing face to face. The knowledge that I have now is imperfect; but then I shall know as fully as I am known. In short, there are

6. McCabe, *God Still Matters*, 8.

three things that last; faith, hope and love; and the greatest of these is love."[7]

This is a beautiful assurance not only for each of us personally but also for our belief in the abiding reality of our loved ones who have died. It is an assurance that, through their faith in God's revelation, these loved ones now consciously enjoy an eternal life of participation in his love. It is a life that we can hope to share with them when we encounter them again in what is felicitously called the communion of saints. For me, it is an assurance that my conviction about the abiding personal reality of my beautiful wife Frankie is well-founded, as indeed is my hope and confidence that we will be together again and will together enjoy the knowledge and experience of God's love for us in what is called the beatific vision. This assurance provides further insight into how my relationship with my beloved and my relationship with God are intimately associated. My confidence in and love of the abiding reality of Frankie's goodness, notwithstanding her physical death, finds confirmation and validation through my faith in the reality of an infinitely good and loving God of which her goodness is a finite cipher.

Having considered briefly in this chapter the remarkable revelation of God's love for us, it is now appropriate to devote attention to achieving some insight into how we should love him. In the following chapter, I will seek to explore briefly what this involves.

7. 1 Cor 13:12–13.

Sixteen

OUR GRACED LOVE OF GOD

The rather meager content of a purely philosophical conception of our requirement to love God is greatly enriched by the disclosure of Christian revelation. At best, the purely philosophical conception centers on the knowledge that we have been created by an infinitely good God to whom we owe our very existence and who enables us to act as the free and rational agents that we are. As such, we can be grateful for his providential care, offer him due veneration, and in a manner love him for his benevolence in our regard. This loving acknowledgment of our status as privileged creatures of a benevolent creator is qualitatively different from the sort of love that a relationship of intimate friendship and equality renders possible.

In Christian teaching, we are positively invoked to love God wholeheartedly. Jesus promises eternal life to those who act according to this requirement. "You must love the Lord your God, with all your heart, with all your soul, with all your strength, and with all your mind, and your neighbor as yourself—do this and life is yours."[1] This is a demanding and unequivocal requirement. In the next chapter I will seek to say something about the associated injunction to love our neighbor. Here, however, I will concentrate

---

1. Lk 10:27–28.

on the clear requirement to love God absolutely and unqualifiedly.

At first sight, this requirement seems beyond the capacity of most of us—with the possible exception of those heroes and heroines of the faith who have been recognized and formally acknowledged as saints. However, we have been assured that we are not simply left to our own resources in responding to this invocation. We are told that we can love God because we have received the Holy Spirit, which is the enabling spirit of God's own love. We can love God because we have been transformed from mere creatures into participants in the love that God is.

How faithfully each one of us exercises our new divinized mode of being depends upon, and is an expression of, our appreciation of this transformation and of our commitment to realizing it in our lives. The sure guide to doing this, we are advised, is to seek to imitate the life of Jesus, whose life embodied the perfect expression of the love of God. "I am the Way, the Truth, and the Life. No one can come to the father except through me."[2]

Learning to love God, with whom we have been graced into a loving relationship of friendship and intimacy, is a lifelong project characterized by various stages. It is a project subject to manifold distractions, failures, and self-indulgent denials of this love. Involving the sacramental life of the Church in our lives is a sustaining way through which we can realize and renew our love of God, which is enabled by the gift of his spirit of love, the Holy Spirit. This dwelling in us of the Holy Spirit enables us to be actively associated with the life of Jesus, which was the most perfect human expression of the love of God the Father.

We can be associated, notwithstanding our manifold failings and denials, with Jesus' salvific life of prayer, fidelity, and selfless

2. Jn 14–16.

conformity to the will of his Father. Through our prayer, participation in the sacraments, and love of neighbor, we can, in however feeble a manner, become associated with Jesus' faithful and unconditional love of God, a love that in his case culminated in his harrowing death upon a cross for our salvation. "The reason he died for all was so that living men should no longer live for themselves, but for him who died and was raised to life for them."[3]

This new life of intimacy and friendship with Jesus in his unconditional love of God, into which we are invited and enabled to participate through God's grace, can be properly viewed as a most remarkable instance of the phenomenon of emergence. Recall again how we describe the distinctive nature of emergence. The fundamental characteristic of emergence is that it obtains as a defining property of an entity that is neither deducible from nor reducible to the properties of the physical components in which it subsists and from which it has emerged. It is not simply a result of the nature, combination, and operation of its constituent components. To describe an entity as emergent is to signify that it obtains and acts in a novel manner, one quite different from the manner in which entities arise naturally, non-controversially, and exclusively as a result of the mere combination of their component parts.

Within the natural order, the emergence of something as the bearer of novel properties and activity may perhaps arise from its component parts as from its necessary material conditions. For example, perhaps when inorganic matter has evolved to a certain level of organic complexity, it attains or obtains a natural capacity to be the subject of the novel emergent realization of physically irreducible rational life. This can be a natural outcome that has evolved from material preconditions, even though what has emerged is es-

3. 2 Cor 5:15.

sentially novel with regard to these preconditions. The outcome of rational life is irreducible to its material preconditions and inexplicable solely in terms of them. Thus one might say that the emergence of the essentially first-person activity of rational thought and action obtains by way of evolution from, but as utterly irreducible to, the essentially third-person nature and character of organically developed material components. What has emerged naturally is irreducibly novel in nature and activity vis-à-vis its necessary and even its sufficient material preconditions. Different and higher orders of intelligibility and being, relating to the emergence of meaning and value rather than just the production of physical motion and interaction, are enabled to come into play. The realm of logical consistency and moral imperative supervenes on the realm of physical interaction and causation.

However, it is certain that the manner in which we have been enabled to love God, by the grace of the Holy Spirit, is not a natural outcome of our constituent components. Our natural constitution, our created nature, may be the necessary but certainly not the sufficient condition of our graced form of life whereby we can love God in a relationship of friendship and intimacy. Grace may presuppose nature but does not emerge from it. Grace is not just a natural occurrence, as appears to be the case with the emergence of rational subjectivity given a specific stage and form of organic development. It is not simply a function of a higher order of *natural* activity, significance, or intelligibility that emerges or supervenes at a certain level of development of its sustaining preconditions. It is a gracious gift, transforming and elevating human nature and enabling a person to exercise an activity of loving friendship with God utterly beyond her intrinsic capacity as a creature. This transforming gift of loving friendship with God, even though compatible with human nature, is quite beyond its intrinsic possibilities. It establishes a new creation, or a new kind or level of creation, that elevates its recipient into an entirely novel form of life as a finite loving participant in God's own life.

One might say that the distinction between our existence simply as wholly dependent creatures endowed with reason and free will and our existence as creatures graced with a capacity for loving participation in God's life accounts for the manner in which we may succeed or fail in fulfilling this capacity to enjoy a loving friendship with God. It is through the self-regarding use of our own reason and free will that we are able to indulge in a way of life that we know to be at odds with and a diversion from our graced invitation to a life of love of God. Our graced capacity to love God is not activated automatically. It requires our conscious and free cooperation in opening ourselves to and exercising the love of God of which we have been made capable. How best this can be done is for each person to discover for herself through her own development of her graced spiritual life. This certainly involves prayer and recourse to the great channels of grace—namely, the sacraments, and notably the Eucharist. However, it cannot be achieved at all without commitment to the other great divine command—namely, to love our neighbor. It is this requirement of love that I wish to consider, however briefly, in the next chapter.

Seventeen

LOVE OF NEIGHBOR

In the scriptures, love of God is inextricably linked with love of one's neighbor. "You must love the Lord your God with all your heart—and your neighbor as yourself."[1] "Anyone who says 'I love God,' and hates his brother, is a liar. Since a man who does not love his brother that he can see cannot love God, whom he has never seen. So this is the commandment that he has given us, that anyone who loves God must also love his brother."[2]

This requirement to love our neighbor goes beyond respect for the rights of all other people and a general benevolence in their regard—although surely it involves this at least. We are required to love others not just in an impersonal egalitarian way but rather "as we love ourselves"! We are expected to treat them as we would wish to be treated and to seek that they may enjoy as full a measure of happiness as we aspire to for ourselves. This is a lofty requirement and one, if we are honest with ourselves, that we honor more in the breach than in the observance. We never, even nearly, measure up to this requirement to love all other people as we love ourselves, and we must rely on the goodness of Christ to supplement our very deficient efforts and to forgive our frequent lapses and activities that

1. Lk 10:27.
2. 1 Jn 4:20–21.

so often run entirely contrary to this commandment's meaning.

Each of us must try to implement this love in the various contexts in which we encounter its appeal. This implementation will vary in expression depending upon whether the object of this loving attention is one's spouse, one's family, one's friends, one's fellow citizens, or the wider community of all humans living and dead. It seems clear that what is required of us is a love that is like the love we have for ourselves and like the love we would wish for from others. This love is intended to be an unselfish, un-self-regarding, non-erotic love that is directed primarily and agapeistically at the wellbeing and fulfillment of our neighbor herself in the various forms in which she may be encountered (e.g., needy, impoverished, lonely, or vulnerable).

However, when one considers the scriptures further, the commandment to love our neighbor seems to go beyond the already demanding requirement to love her as we love ourselves and would wish to be loved. Jesus urges us to love one another not just as we love ourselves and would wish to be loved but as he has loved us. "This is my commandment: love one another, as I have loved you. A man can have no greater love than to lay down his life for his friends."[3]

Here we have to acknowledge that we are invoked beyond the "golden rule" of love of our neighbor, which is at least comprehensible and a reasonable expectation (even though we habitually fall far short of it). We are asked to love our neighbor in a manner that is quite beyond any natural requirement. In saying that this is beyond any natural requirement, I am not denying the beautiful and self-disregarding loving actions of the many wonderful people, often convinced atheists, who in various and often terrifying

3. Jn 15:13–14.

circumstances have laid down their lives for love of their neighbor. However, it would be difficult to argue that this action is a norm or one that is naturally required of us.

To love our neighbor as Christ has loved us is quite beyond what might be naturally expected of us and quite beyond our natural capacity and customary practice. And yet it is commanded of us. It is a command whose fulfillment can be made possible only through the grace of God, which enables us, despite much failure on our parts, to participate in a limited way in Christ's own love of us.

This reassurance is vividly and reassuringly portrayed in the beautiful scriptural imagery of our transformed state as branches of the vine that is Christ. "I am the vine; you are the branches. Whoever remains in me, with me in him, bears fruit in plenty; for cut off from me you can do nothing."[4] Here Jesus is revealed as the source of the new love of which we are capable. We are made capable, in however imperfect a way, of loving our neighbor as Jesus has loved us because we are enlivened by his life and love. In this endeavor we are greatly encouraged by the remarkable love of neighbor expressed by heroes of the faith, such as Augustine, Francis, Vincent de Paul, Thérèse, Maximilian Kolbe. We can envisage our neighbor as participating with us in the life of Christ. In our experience of our neighbor's dereliction in various forms, we can envisage and respond to him or her as representing the suffering body of Christ himself.

If we acknowledge the commandment to love our neighbor as Christ has loved us, we should reflect upon how this acknowledgment implies that we are capable, in however imperfect a manner, of acting in accordance with this requirement. This reflection discloses that we have been enabled to act in a manner that quite

4. Jn 15:5.

exceeds our natural capacity simply as creatures. We have been enabled to operate in a novel manner relative to our natural capacities, enabled to live as finite but genuine participants in God's own life of infinite love.

How, and in what measure, each of us seeks, or declines, to live in accordance with his or her graced capacity to live this enhanced form of life is a personal responsibility. The responsibility can and does take myriad forms corresponding to the individual circumstances and dedication of each person—lay or religious, celibate or married, healthy or ill, richly endowed or impoverished.

An important consideration to bear in mind is that this enhanced form of life can be viewed as an instance of the phenomenon of emergence to which I have alluded in various contexts throughout this reflection. Emergence renders possible a novel level of activity, one neither reducible to nor deducible from our capacity considered as simply creatures in abstraction from our graced lives. In the concluding chapter, I will try to bring together various strands of this discussion of emergence with particular reference to its bearing on the central preoccupation of my reflection about love of God and love of my neighbor—a neighbor most intimately represented for me in the person of my beautiful wife.

Eighteen

CONCLUDING REFLECTION

Love of God and love of neighbor summarize what Christian faith both enables us to do and requires of us. In each case the love invoked involves more than might be discovered by natural reason. What is proposed to us about love by Christian faith enhances remarkably what we might discover about it through our own natural reason independent of this divine revelation. But this faith presupposes and does not contradict what we might discover through philosophical discussion and reflection about the nature of love of both God and neighbor.

What is characteristic of both love of God and of neighbor is the phenomenon of emergence, a guiding theme throughout this reflection. As Elly Vitandis has indicated, by way of a definition of emergence "we could say that a property is emergent if it is a novel property of a system or entity that arises when that system or entity has reached a certain level of complexity and that, although it exists only insofar as the system or entity exists, it is distinct from the properties of the parts of the system from which it emerges."[1] Moreover, where such an emergent property obtains, the system or

1. Elly Vintiadis, "Emergence," in *The Internet Encyclopedia of Philosophy*, 1996, https://www.iep.utm.edu.

entity manifests a novel and unique form of activity that cannot be derived from and is irreducible to the properties of its parts.

It seems clear that the natural love of neighbor can and does involve an exercise of our subjectivity that it is quite impossible to explain exclusively in impersonal physical terms. At times this love can undoubtedly be primarily physical in its motivation and also even quite selfish in its intention. However, even such mainly self-regarding instances of love of neighbor involve a level of conscious awareness and intentional involvement that are quite irreducible to the physical organization of the component parts of the organic system that sustains them. The emergent character of love is most obvious in those instances of love that are primarily directed not to one's own satisfaction but intentionally and unselfishly to the intrinsic lovable goodness of the beloved. Undoubtedly, even this intentional and unselfish love of the intrinsic goodness of the neighbor is usually directed to their incarnate physical reality and resonates effectively in the incarnate physical reality of the lover. But it is clearly an exercise of a level of personal subjectivity that cannot be translated without residue into physicochemical terms.

Even more remarkable is the emergent character evidenced by one's love of the intrinsic lovable goodness of a deceased beloved, who is loved not just as a treasured memory but as an existing disincarnate reality. Such love, if it is not a delusion, manifests a quality of emergence and transcendence of the physical limits of one's reality—an emergence that cannot be reformulated reductively in exclusively physical terms. Moreover, this love expresses a love of one's beloved as someone who is envisaged and loved as truly existing in a manner no longer pertaining to the physical condition that is characteristic of our incarnate human reality.

How such a love, if it is what it claims to be, might be analyzed reductively as only a physical process seems to me to be a futile and misconceived initiative. Because such reductive analysis is unsatisfactory, one may be tempted to choose what might seem a simpler, safer, and more comprehensible option—namely, to deem that such love is a delusion. Perhaps it is only a heartbroken mistaken identification of one's beloved as an existing person when in reality she is only a poignant memory. Perhaps it is more appropriate to interpret such a claim to know and love the existence of what is certainly not given in sensible perception as a deception, an exercise in self-deception or wish fulfillment.

Other misgivings can extend the uncertainty that this possibility engenders. For example, if I am so lovingly committed to the ongoing personal existence of my beloved, why do I not experience her presence as a directly perceived awareness or evidence of the loving reality that I claim her to be? Could it be that my commitment to her ongoing personal existence is an illusion by means of which I seek to transform a cherished memory into an alleged existing reality? Am I perhaps unwilling or unable to accept the harsh truth that she no longer exists?

However, before acceding to this supposedly more plausible account, it is worth recalling Soren Kierkegaard's remark on the issue:

If it were true—as conceited shrewdness, proud of not being deceived, thinks—that one should believe nothing which he cannot see by means of his physical eyes, then first and foremost one ought to give up believing in love. If one did this out of fear of being deceived, would not one then be deceived? Indeed one can be deceived in many ways; one can be deceived in believing what is untrue, but on the other hand, one is also deceived in not believing what is true.... To cheat oneself out of love is the most terrible deception; it is an eternal loss for which there is no reparation, either in time or in eternity.[2]

This reflection by Kierkegaard about how one may be deceived by not believing what may be true is profound and very thought-provoking. It highlights how an impoverished conception of what may count as truth can undermine belief in the reality of love. It reminds me of a personal conviction, reached when I was much younger, that part of the deep meaning of what I say in declaring to someone "I love YOU unconditionally" is that "you will not die."

Undoubtedly this assertion flies in the face of empirical evidence, but nevertheless I believe it to be true. When I say "I love you" to my beloved, I am certainly not looking on her as just the accidental combination of material atoms, however beautiful, that she is and that will inevitably someday disperse and scatter. I am saying that my love of her affirms more about her and her significance for me than that. And it is this unique, profoundly mysterious, more than just material reality that she is that evokes my love for her. My lived experience of her goodness, disclosed in her invisible loving gaze upon me, originates and sustains my love for her. In her unselfish loving gaze, I experience her goodness as an abiding value, illuminating her physical beauty but not reducible to it. It draws me out of myself, out of my selfishness, to cherish her unreservedly. It enables me to say to my beloved Frankie "I love you" and mean thereby that for me "you will never die—for I have been privileged to know that in you which transcends your physical beauty."

However, although one may thus maintain one's love for one's beloved as love of her abiding "spiritual" reality, as existing be-

2. Soren Kierkegaard, *Works of Love*, trans. Howard and Edna Hong (New York: Harper, 2009), 23–24.

yond the sphere of her previous incarnate existence, there remains a profound question about how this can be so in terms of purely rational speculation. The claim to know that one's beloved really exists in this disincarnate spiritual way appears to be very much an initiative of faith as well as of reason, perhaps a rational faith inspired by a loving hope. It would seem that if one is to achieve an ultimate foundation and convincing vindication of such an affirmation of the abiding existence of one's beloved, an affirmation of the free and sustaining love of an infinitely good God is required. Could it be that the logic of faith resembles a view through an opaque one-way window, a commitment that must be renewed until I experience the joy of eternal life in communion with my beautiful wife and all of those beloved ones who I will love in the sustaining knowledge and friendship of an infinitely good and loving God?

Here one might be reminded of the Platonic explanation of all particular expressions of goodness as participations in a supreme exemplar idea of goodness. However, the Platonic exemplar ideas are inert and inactive and incapable of willing anything. What is required by the claim that I have been considering is the existence of a personal infinite goodness who actually wills and consciously sustains in abiding love the continued disincarnate existence of those we love. This loving faith in the ongoing personal reality of our loved ones can serve as a cipher that may perhaps, either through rational argument or Christian faith, be deciphered by the affirmation of a loving and infinitely good God. This affirmation of a loving God, in turn, provides an ultimate foundation, explanation, and vindication of the affirmation of the continued disincarnate life of those whom we love. A circular reflection perhaps but not, I believe, a contradiction.

The loving affirmation of the continued existence of my beloved is more than the conclusion of an impersonal rational argument. It certainly involves a rational claim that she is more existentially significant than the dust into which her mortal physical body has been dissolved. But this rational intimation is transformed into an assured belief in her continued personal existence by the loving affirmation of my intellect and the loving adhesion of my will to the more than simply physical desirability or goodness that she signifies for me. Further, the affirmation of a loving God, to whom this belief appeals as its condition and foundation, is an extended affirmation of what might be called my rational faith that ultimately goodness prevails over the absurdity of contingent circumstance. By this I mean that the rationality of a loving hope is the basis for acknowledging that what is intrinsically good and lovable is how reality ultimately is—that a commitment to the ultimate reality of goodness, truth, and beauty is not just a deception, or a great illusion. It is a rational conviction that what *should* be the case (because intrinsically good and desirable) ultimately *is* the case or, in more technical terms, that what is reasonably affirmed as axiologically or morally desirable ultimately coincides with what is ontologically real, with how things truly and ultimately are.

It seems to me that it is this intuition—that what should be so is how things really are—that motivates St. Anselm's contention, mentioned earlier, that what can be envisaged as better and more desirable that any finite goodness that we might conceive must really exist. The same line of reflection, as we also saw, can be found in the thought of Immanuel Kant. Although notoriously skeptical about impersonal metaphysical arguments about the existence of God, he nevertheless argued that in moral considerations it is rational to hope in and to affirm a personal belief in God envisaged as rationally desirable infinite goodness.

Thus, although in a much more modest way, my reflection on love—love of my beautiful wife Frankie and its associated love of God—echoes the conviction of Anselm and Kant that we can hopefully but rationally affirm that the good we lovingly value and desire is congruent with how things ultimately are. In my case, this means that my loving trust in Frankie's continued personal existence and in the existence of a loving God as the ultimate vindication of this trust is not just a fond wish but a reasonable and reliable belief in accordance with how things actually are, a belief confirmed by faith in the salvific life, death, and resurrection of Jesus.

The concept that sustains this hopeful reflection and that resists the contemporary tendency to prioritize a reductive explanation of all experience is the concept of emergence. On several occasions throughout this reflection, I have described emergence as a property of a system or entity that is neither deducible from nor reducible to the properties and interaction of its component parts and that exercises a novel activity on these components and upon its environment.

I indicated that characteristic human properties such as consciousness, reason, and will are properly understood as emergent relative to the biological context in which they subsist. I argued that the remarkable phenomenon of love is even more assuredly an emergent property wherever it obtains—except in that unique and infinite divine reality in which it is not emergent but rather with which it is identical. God's love is not an emergent property. God is love—a love that renders all other emergent love possible.

Emergent human love expresses a person's self-conscious, rational, and voluntary reaching out towards another who is perceived and valued as a personal goodness to be cherished. This personal goodness, or other person, can be loved and valued either

erotically, as fulfilling one's own needs and desires, or more intentionally, selflessly, and agapeistically for her own self-possessed
intrinsic goodness and beauty.

It makes little sense to try to explain this emergent phenomenon
of human love reductively in terms of physics and chemistry, even
though this love certainly emerges from a structured physical organism in which it subsists. The natural world in which such love obtains
must be understood to include various levels of emergent meaning
and value that obtain beyond the domains of physical, chemical, and
biological reality, and in which appropriately developed or evolved
physical organisms can participate. It seems as though the natural
world of our experience lends itself or is led to an emergent development of meaning and value of which selfless human love is the
highest expression. From this perspective, one's rational hope in the
disincarnate continued existence of one's loved one is affirmed. As
thus existing, she can be loved both for herself and as a revealing
cipher of the loving God who sustains her in existence.

We have seen earlier how this rational hope and faith in the
continued existence of one's beloved, sustained by the love of God,
are given remarkable confirmation and development in Christian
revelation. Here the human condition is elevated to a level beyond
the resources of the natural order. It is raised to divinely graced
life, to a new kind of being in which one is enabled to participate,
with one's beloved and others, in the love that is God's life.

One can speak analogically of this new graced life as an emergent reality. However, unlike other cases of emergence, this new
graced life is not a matter of attaining a new irreducible level of
being for which one has a natural, though created, active capacity.
The emergence into graced participation in God's own life is not
a natural outcome, as are other instances of emergence, from our

condition as creatures of a specific kind. This graced emergence is not like our natural emergence into rational life from the material context of our characteristically human physical organization. It is a gracious gift which comes to us from God himself, enabling us to enter into loving friendship with him. It is an emergence from mere creaturehood into friendship with God.

Perhaps this emergent gracious gift of friendship with God might be more appropriately called "advenience" rather than "emergence." This designation would emphasize that we are talking about a novel way of being and acting that, although it presupposes our creaturely condition, is entirely beyond any natural capacity of this condition. This way of life comes to us as a gracious gift rather than as any new emergent status of which we may be naturally capable.

Perhaps also this "advenient" or "coming to be as gracious gift" form of emergence may shed deeper light on the other natural forms of human emergence that we have mentioned, such as the natural emergence of consciousness, reason, free will, and love. Perhaps they too should be considered retrospectively not just as forms of natural emergence, which can be affirmed initially without any reference to their created origin. They can also, and more fundamentally, be recognized as "advenient" forms of a loving gift, which characterize them as pertaining to the lovingly created natural world that we humans inhabit. Thus, fundamentally, our specially graced emergence into God's love and friendship is not the only advenient gift. Perhaps also our various forms of natural emergence, such as our incarnate conscious subjectivity, our reason, will, and love, when understood ultimately as enabled features of God's creation, can also be described analogically as advenient forms of God's love for us.

From such a perspective, all manifestations of emergence can be viewed as evidence of the love God has for us in enabling us to exist as creatures of a natural order capable of emergent activities of reason, will, and love and on the basis of which he makes available to us the further gracious gift of active participation in his own love. What is spoken of as simply a natural phenomenon of emergence prior to any knowledge of God takes on a new significance when this natural order of things is known to be a divinely bestowed gift that enables us to exist and to act in the various irreducible ways in which we do. From such a perspective, the various enigmatic forms and levels of natural emergence that characterize us can be seen in a new light as remarkable advenient gifts coming to us as creatures of a loving God. They provide the presupposition of the gift of divine grace, which enables us to participate in God's own love.

A further advantage of designating even the various forms of natural emergence as advenient is that this designation explicitly precludes the suggestion that the novelty referred to in the definition of emergence might refer only to our present incapacity to comprehend how any alleged instance of emergence might, in fact, have been wholly caused by its component physical parts. This could leave open the supposition that emergence might signify only an epistemological characteristic. If this were so, emergence would refer only to our current *incapacity* to explain the emergent novelty in terms of prior natural efficient causality rather than to *an objective reality* establishing radical ontological novelty and difference irreducible to any explanation in terms of natural prior causality. Describing natural emergence from the perspective of creation as an advenient gift of God precludes it from being seen as merely an epi-phenomenon—that is, a poorly understood byproduct of physical causes (such as a person's shadow) with no distinctive independent reality or activity.

From this perspective, which understands the remarkable reality of emergence (both natural and graciously enabled) as advenient gift of God, I find confirmation of the rational hope that motivated this reflection—namely, that I am not deluded in my love of my beautiful Frankie as still alive, nor in my love of a gracious and loving God who enabled this to be how things truly are. In the final analysis, I am truly able to love her and to love God not only in virtue of my naturally emergent and divinely created natural capacity to love. In virtue of the advenient gift of the Holy Spirit (which is the spirit of divine love), I am also enabled to love her and to love God in a more than naturally enabled way. I and she have been graciously enabled to participate together in the love that God is. I can celebrate at present an "Advent" of a future together in the love of God, a future that I can now confidently and joyfully anticipate. Through my Christian faith, I can affirm that this joyful anticipation is more than a reasonable hope. I can confidently affirm that this is how it will be—that THIS IS WHAT IT ALL ULTIMATELY MEANS.

Bibliography

Aquinas, Thomas. *Summa contra Gentiles: On the Truth of the Catholic Faith.*
 Translated by Anton Pegis, J. F. Anderson, V. J. Bourke, and C. J. O'Neill.
 New York: Doubleday, 1955–57.
———. *Summa theologiae.* Translated by the English Dominicans. London:
 Eyre and Spottiswoode, 1964–74.
Aristotle. *Generation of Animals.* Translated by A. L. Peck. Cambridge, Mass.:
 Harvard University Press, 1942.
Augustine. *Contra Faustum.* Vol. 4 of *Nicene and Post-Nicene Fathers, First
 Series,* edited by Philip Schaff. Buffalo, N.Y: Christian Literature
 Publishing, 1887.
Bacon, Francis. *De Augmentis Scientarum.* Cambridge: Cambridge University
 Press, 2011.
Baggott, Jim. *A Beginner's Guide to Reality.* London: Penguin Books, 2005.
Barth, Karl. *The Epistle to the Romans.* Translated by Edwyn C. Hosykns.
 Oxford: Oxford University Press, 1933.
Benedict XVI. *Deus Caritas Est.* Encyclical Letter. December 25, 2005.
Caputo, John and Gianni Vattimo. *After the Death of God.* New York: Columbia
 University Press, 2007.
Comte, Auguste. *The Positive Philosophy of Auguste Comte.* Translated and
 condensed by Harriet Martineau. 2 vols. London: Chapman, 1853.
Flew, Antony. *God and Philosophy.* London: Hutchinson, 1966.
Geach, Peter. *Reason and Argument.* Oxford: Oxford University Press, 1976.
Gilson, Etienne. *The Unity of Philosophical Experience.* San Francisco: Ignatius
 Press, 1999.
Haldane, John. "Philosophy Lives." *First Things* 209 (January 2011): 43–46.
Harre, Rom. *Philosophies of Science.* Oxford: Oxford University Press, 1970.
Hassing, Richard. "Modern Natural Science and the Intelligibility of Being."
 In *Final Causality in Nature and Human Affairs,* edited by Hassing, 211–56.
 Washington, D.C.: The Catholic University of America Press, 1997.

Heaney, Seamus. *The Redress of Poetry*. London: Faber and Faber, 1995.

Hegel, G. F. *Encyclopaedia Logic*. Translated by William Wallace. Oxford: Oxford University Press, 1892.

———. *Lectures on the Philosophy of Religion*, vol. 1. Translated by Peter C. Hodgson. Berkeley: University of California Press, 1984.

Husserl, Edmund. *Ideas: General Introduction to Pure Phenomenology*. Translated by W. Boyce Gibson. New York: Collier Books, 1962.

———. *The Crisis of European Sciences and Transcendental Phenomenology*. Translated by David Carr. Evanston, Ill.: Northwestern University Press, 1970.

Kant, Immanuel. *Critique of Practical Reason*, 6th ed. Translated by Thomas K. Abbott. London: Longmans, 1909.

———. *Religion within the Limits of Reason Alone*. Translated by Theodore M. Greene and Hoyt H. Hudson. New York: Harper Torchbooks, 1960.

———. *Critique of Pure Reason*. Translated by N. Kemp Smith. London: Macmillan, 1968.

Kaufmann, Stuart. *At Home in the Universe*. London: Viking Press, 1995.

Kearney, Richard. *The God Who May Be*. Bloomington: Indiana University Press, 2001.

———. *Reimagining the Sacred*. Edited by Kearney and Jens Zimmermann. New York: Columbia University Press, 2016.

Kenny, Anthony. "The Argument from Design." In *Reason and Religion: Essays in Philosophical Theology*. Oxford: Blackwell, 1987.

Kierkegaard, Soren. *Concluding Unscientific Postscript*. Translated by David Swenson and Walter Lowrie. Princeton: Princeton University Press, 1941.

———. *Works of Love*. Translated by Howard and Edna Hong. New York: Harper, 2009.

Ladriere, Jean. *Les enjeux de la rationalité: Le défi de la science et de la technologie aux cultures*. Paris: Aubier-Montaigne, 1977.

Levinas, Emmanuel. *Totality and Infinity*. Translated by Alphonso Lingis. Pittsburgh: Duquesne University Press, 1969.

Lyas, Colin. "The Groundlessness of Religious Belief." In *Reason and Religion*, edited by Stuart C. Brown, 158–80. Ithaca, N.Y.: Cornell University Press, 1977.

Malcolm, Norman. "The Groundlessness of Belief" in *Reason and Religion*, edited by Stuart C. Brown, 143–57. Ithaca, N.Y.: Cornell University Press, 1977.

Marion, Jean-Luc. *Cartesian Questions: Method and Metaphysics*. Translated and edited by Jeffrey Kosky. Chicago: University of Chicago Press, 1999.

———. *God, the Gift, and Postmodernism*. Edited by John D. Caputo and Michael J. Scanlon. Bloomington: Indiana University Press, 1999.

———. "The Event, the Phenomenon and the Revealed." In *Transcendence in Philosophy and Religion*, edited by James E. Faulconer, 87–105. Bloomington: Indiana University Press, 2003.

———. *The Visible and the Revealed*. Translated by Christina Gschwandtner et al. New York: Fordham University Press, 2008.

Marx, Karl. *Contribution to the Critique of Hegel's Philosophy of Right: Early Writings*. Translated by T. B. Bottomore. London: C. A. Watts, 1963.

Masterson, Patrick. "The Arts Degree in an Age of Science and Technology." *The Crane Bag* 7, no. 2 (1983): 33–40.

———. *Approaching God: Between Phenomenology and Theology*. New York: Bloomsbury, 2013.

McCabe, Herbert. *God Still Matters*. London: Continuum, 2002.

McConnell, David. "Why Science Has Made Humanism Inevitable." Address to the Humanist Association of Ireland, Dublin, July 3, 2016. https://www.humanism.ie/2016/06/first-sunday-meeting-july-3-2016/.

Meillassoux, Quentin. *After Finitude: An Essay on the Necessity of Contingency*. Translated by Ray Brassier. London: Continuum, 2008.

Merleau-Ponty, Maurice. *Eloge de la philosophie*. Paris: Gallimard, 1958.

———. "Le Métaphysique dans l'homme." In *Sens et non-sens*, 3rd ed., 145–71. Paris: Gallimard, 1961.

Murdoch, Iris. *The Sovereignty of Good*. London: Routledge and Kegan Paul, 1970.

Nagel, Thomas. *The Possibility of Altruism*. Oxford: Clarendon Press, 1970.

———. *Mind and Cosmos: Why the Materialist Neo-Darwinian Conception of Nature Is Almost Certainly False*. Oxford: Oxford University Press, 2011.

Philips, D. Z. *Faith and Philosophical Enquiry*. London: Routledge and Kegan Paul, 1970.

Plato. *Symposium*. In *The Dialogues of Plato*. Translated by Benjamin Jowett. New York: Random House, 1937.

Ricoeur, Paul. "Experience and Language in Religious Discourse." In

Phenomenology and the Theological Turn: The French Debate, edited by Janicaud Dominique, translated by Bernard G. Prusak and Jeffrey L. Kosky. New York: Fordham University Press, 2000.

Ross, James. "Christians Get the Best of Evolution." In *Evolution and Creation*, edited by Ernan McMullin, 223–51. Notre Dame, Ind.: Notre Dame University Press, 1985.

Russell, Bertrand. "A Free Man's Worship." In *Mysticism and Logic and Other Essays*, 36–44. London: George Allen and Unwin, 1917.

Sartre, Jean-Paul. *The Flies*. Translated by Stuart Gilbert. New York: Knopf, 1947.

———. "Cartesian Freedom." In *Literary and Philosophical Essays*, translated by Annette Michelson. London: Hutchinson, 1969.

Scheler, Max. *Ressentiment*. Translated by William W. Holdheim. New York: Schoken Books, 1972.

Smith, John. *Experience and God*. Oxford: Oxford University Press, 1968.

Sokolowski, Robert. *Christian Faith and Human Understanding*. Washington, D.C.: The Catholic University of America Press, 2006.

Stace, W. T. *A Critical History of Greek Philosophy*. London: Macmillan, 1967.

Van Riet, Georges. *Philosophie et religion*. Paris: Editions Beatrice Nauwelaerts, 1970.

Vatican Council I. *Dei Filius* II. Dogmatic Constitution. April 24, 1870.

Vintiadis, Elly. "Emergence." In *The Internet Encyclopedia of Philosophy*. https://www.iep.utm.edu.

Weil, Simone. *First and Last Notebooks*. Translated by Rush Rees. London: Oxford University Press, 1970.

Winch, Peter. "Meaning and Religious Language." In *Reason and Religion*, edited by Stuart C. Brown, 193–221. Ithaca, N.Y.: Cornell University Press, 1977.

Wittgenstein, Ludwig. *Tractatus logico-philosophicus*. London: Routledge and Kegan Paul, 1922.

Zahavi, Dan. "Phenomenology." In *The Routledge Companion to Twentieth Century Philosophy*, edited by Dermot Moran, 670–79. London: Routledge, 2008.

Index

In Reasonable Hope: Philosophical Reflections on Ultimate Meaning
was designed in Filosofia and composed by Kachergis Book Design of
Pittsboro, North Carolina. It was printed on 60-pound House Natural
Smooth Web and bound by Sheridan Books of Chelsea, Michigan.